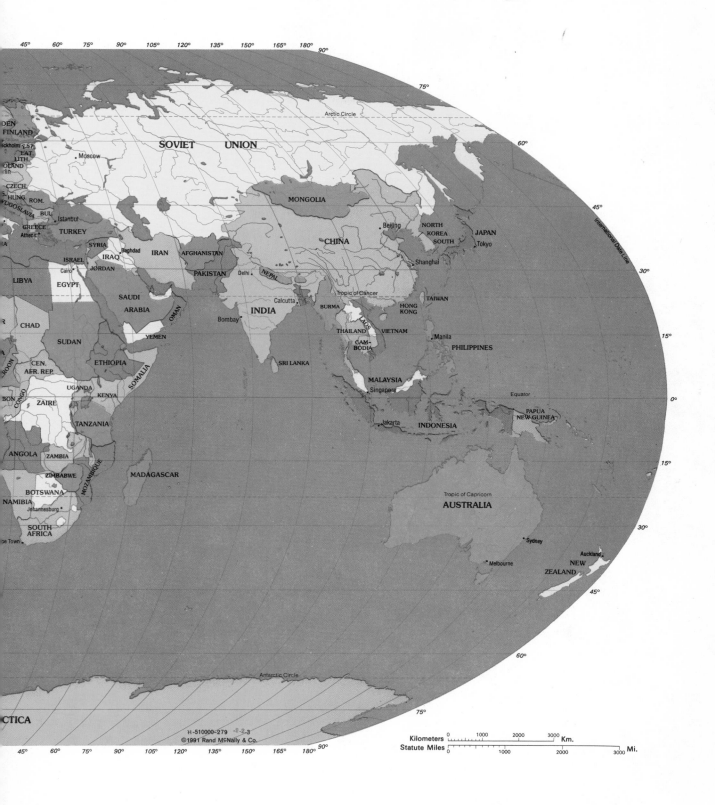

Young Students World Atlas

NEWFIELD
PUBLICATIONS

MIDDLETOWN · CONNECTICUT

Contents

At the time of printing the Soviet Union had been dissolved. The former republics of the Soviet Union are now independent states. The map on pages 30–31 shows the extent of the new states. The name, Soviet Union, has been retained as a point of reference only.

PHOTO CREDITS:

Satellite photographs on pages 10 – 15 from *Images of the World* © 1983 by Rand McNally & Company. Originally published in German under the title of DIERCKE WELTRAUMBILD-ATLAS. Copyright © 1981 by Georg Westermann Verlag, Braunschweig/Federal Republic of Germany.

Revised Edition, 1992

ISBN 0-8374-0493-2

Library of Congress Catalog Card Number: 87-51144

The *Young Students World Atlas* has been prepared especially for Newfield Publications, Inc. by Rand McNally & Company

Young Students Learning Library is a federally registered trademark of Newfield Publications, Inc.

Printed in the United States of America

The Earth in Space

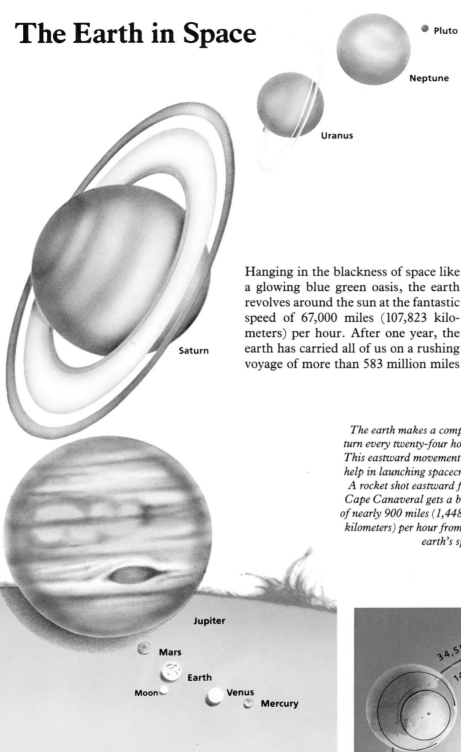

Pluto

Neptune

Uranus

Saturn

Jupiter

Mars

Earth

Moon

Venus

Mercury

Hanging in the blackness of space like a glowing blue green oasis, the earth revolves around the sun at the fantastic speed of 67,000 miles (107,823 kilometers) per hour. After one year, the earth has carried all of us on a rushing voyage of more than 583 million miles (938,221,900 kilometers)! The earth is a spacecraft taking us on a journey around the sun.

In addition to orbiting the sun, the earth makes a rapid rotating movement on its axis. Each earth day is a result of one rotation. Once every twenty-four hours, the earth turns completely around. As it does so, the sun seems to slip across the sky, rising in the east and setting in the west. But the sun is not moving. It is the earth whirling itself about like a merry-go-round that causes what seems to be the sun's motion.

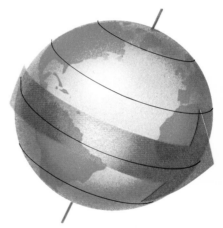

The earth makes a complete turn every twenty-four hours. This eastward movement is a help in launching spacecraft. A rocket shot eastward from Cape Canaveral gets a boost of nearly 900 miles (1,448.37 kilometers) per hour from the earth's spin.

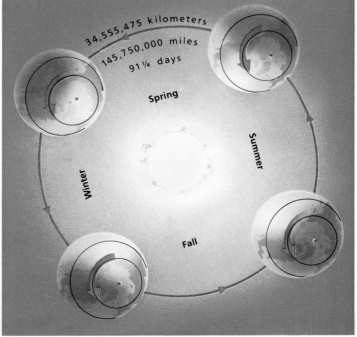

34,555,475 kilometers
145,750,000 miles
91¼ days

Spring

Summer

Winter

Fall

The 23½° tilt of the earth's axis and the earth's yearly trip around the sun cause the seasons. In summer, the northern part of the earth is tipped toward the sun, receiving more heat. In spring and fall, both parts of the globe receive equal amounts of sunlight. In winter, the northern part is tipped away from the sun and therefore receives less heat. It is all a matter of angles, not distance. In fact, the earth is a little closer to the sun when January blizzards howl across Europe and North America than when the July thermometer pokes past 100°F (38°C).

NEPTUNE
Dia. 27,700 mi.
44,600 km.
Rot. 18.5 hrs.
Dist. from Sun 2,794,190,000 mi.
4,496,600,000 km.
Rev. 164.8 yrs.
Moons 2

JUPITER
Dia. 88,700 mi.
142,700 km.
Rot. 9.92 hrs.
Dist. from Sun 483,700,000 mi.
778,400,000 km.
Rev. 11.86 yrs.
Moons 16
Rings 1
Dia. 160,300 mi.
258,000 km.

EARTH
Dia. 7,926 mi.
12,756 km.
Rot. 23.93 hrs.
Dist. from Sun 92,960,000 mi.
149,600,000 km.
Rev. 365.26 days
Moons 1

Comet

MERCURY
Dia. 3,032 mi.
4,878 km.
Rot. 58.65 days
Dist. from Sun 35,980,000 mi.
57,900,000 km.
Rev. 88 days

MARS
Dia. 4,212 mi.
6,778 km.
Rot. 24.62 hr
Dist. from Su
Rev. 1.88 yrs
Moons 2

VENUS
Dia. 7,520 mi.
12,104 km.
Rot. 243.1 days
Dist. from Sun 67,240,000 mi.
108,200,000 km.
Rev. 224.7 days

SUN
Dia. 865,000 mi.
1,392,000 km.
Rot. 25.4 days
Surf. Temp. 5,800° Kelvin
Cen. Temp 15,000,000° Kelvin

M-33 Galaxy

PLUTO
Dia. 1,860 mi.
3,000 km.
Rot. 6.39 days
Dist. from Sun 3,706,780,000 mi.
5,965,200,000 km.

Rev. 247 yrs.
Moons 1

URANUS
Dia. 32,600 mi.
52,400 km.
Rot. 16 hrs.
Dist. from Sun 1,783,170,000 mi.
2,869,600,000 km.

Rev. 84.01 yrs.
Moons 5
Rings 9
Dia. 59,700 mi.
96,000 km.

Map of Outer Space

Our solar system is part of the Milky Way galaxy, which is represented on the map by the blue area. The yellow lines show each planet's path of orbit, and the small light-colored spheres found near most of the planets are moons. The purplish bodies below Jupiter are asteroids.

ABBREVIATIONS

Dia. :   Diameter of planet
Rot. :   Planet rotation time
Dist. from Sun :
          Distance from the sun
Rev. :   Revolution time around
          the sun

SATURN
Dia. 75,100 mi.
121,000 km.
Rot. 10.67 hrs.
Dist. from Sun 886,740,000 mi.
1,427,000,000 km.

Rev. 29.46 yrs.
Moons 21, possibly 23
Ring System
More than 1,000 ringlike
features in 6 distinct bands
Dia. 177,100 mi.
285,000 km.

Andromeda Galaxy

On its voyage around the sun, the earth is accompanied by eight other planets—plus asteroids, comets, meteoroids, and dust. The sun and the bodies revolving around it make up the solar system. Our solar system is a tiny part of one of the millions of galaxies, or groups of stars, that form the universe.

The center of the solar system, the sun is actually a star. Its gravitational pull holds the solar system together. It keeps the earth and the other planets from flinging themselves into the starry reaches of outer space.

Our planet is a pygmy among the giants of the solar system. Mighty Jupiter could form more than 300 earths! But the earth is far more solid than the bigger planets. Neptune and Uranus are little more than thick gas balls. Saturn is so light it could float in water. Jupiter is only a little heavier than water.

None of these other planets can support life as we know it. Most contain choking gases. The planets closest to the sun, such as Mercury and Venus, are sizzling hot. The planets far away from the sun, like Neptune and Pluto, are cold as tombstones. On a hot day on Venus, temperatures can reach 900°F (482°C), and the surface of Saturn is −285°F (−176°C).

Our planet is neither too close nor too far from the life-giving sun. The earth alone has scarlet flowers and swaying trees and creatures that laugh and cry and care for one another. It is the jewel of the solar system.

Mapping the World

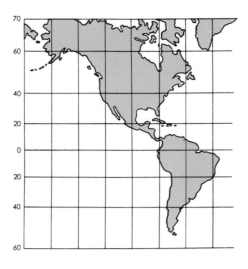

If a globe is projected onto a cylinder, it is called a cylindrical projection.

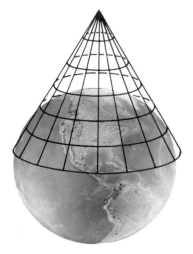

Projection of the globe onto a cone results in a conic projection.

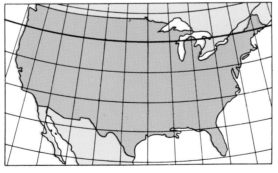

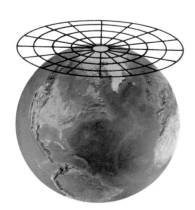

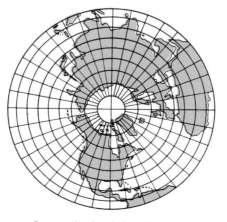

Plane-surface projection is based upon the projection of the globe onto a disc.

Where in the world am I? Have you ever looked at a map to discover just where you are in the world? And why a map?

A map makes it possible to understand where we are in relation to other people and places. Without maps, our understanding of the world would be limited to what we can see. A map is the best way to communicate information about the earth's surface.

The most accurate model of the earth is a globe. However, a globe doesn't show much detail of the earth. Nor is a globe easy to store in a drawer or carry around in your pocket. A flat map can have many details and is easy to carry or store. And a map can show large areas on a single piece of paper, making it easy to compare cities, countries, and other places.

But how can the curved surface of the globe be transformed into a flat map? Cartographers have found the answer, called map projection.

Map Projections

Most maps contain lines that cross to form a grid. These lines are called parallels of latitude and meridians of longitude. (For a more detailed description of latitude and longitude, see the section "Using the Atlas.") Transforming the round earth into a flat surface is done by projecting this grid onto a simple shape, such as a cylinder, a cone, or a plane shaped like a disc. The surface is then flattened, and the transformation has taken place. The round earth is on flat paper.

This is done in much the same way as a picture is projected onto a movie screen. Or think of a light inside a transparent globe, projecting the grid lines of the globe onto paper, where they can be traced.

However, each projection has some distortion. On a flat surface, it is impossible to represent the angles, distance, direction, and area that only a globe can faithfully show.

Experiment with this yourself. Peel an orange carefully and lay the orange peel on a flat surface. The peel will distort as you flatten it out.

While there is distortion in map projections, the places in the world are always in the right location on a map. The grid of latitude and longitude guarantees this accuracy.

There are many different kinds of map projections, and each is used to show specific features for a specific purpose. Often the type of projection is listed somewhere on the map. At the bottom of the physical-political maps and the environment maps in this atlas, the type of projection is stated.

But once the outline of the earth is on flat paper, how does the cartographer get information to fill in the map? One way is through satellite imagery.

Imagery and Maps

For thousands of years, people have been trying to get a bird's-eye view of the earth. At one time, they climbed trees or hills to get a better view of the terrain around them.

Modern technology has found a way for us to see more of our world than we can with the naked eye or a telescope. Today, there are satellites and airplanes circling the earth, equipped with cameras and electronic equipment acting as "remote sensors."

From a distance, remote sensors gather and record information about features on the earth. The cameras' sensitive film and the electronic instruments are so highly developed that they can detect things that our eyes cannot see. The pictures and information gathered by these satellites and airplanes are used by cartographers to create detailed, up-to-date maps.

Some of the best examples of remotely sensed imagery are the pictures gathered by the Landsat satellites. These satellites were launched in 1972, 1975, and 1978. As the Landsat satellites pass over the land taking pictures, information about water, soil, vegetation, and crops is sent back to earth. Every eighteen days, each satellite orbits over the same area, so that changes in the terrain can be detected. As a result, the satellite images show changes in crop, vegetation, and farming patterns; damage resulting from hurricanes, earthquakes, floods, and fires; erosion patterns; desert sand movements; and other changes that

An aircraft-mounted camera produced this high-altitude photograph of the Goodland, Kansas, area.

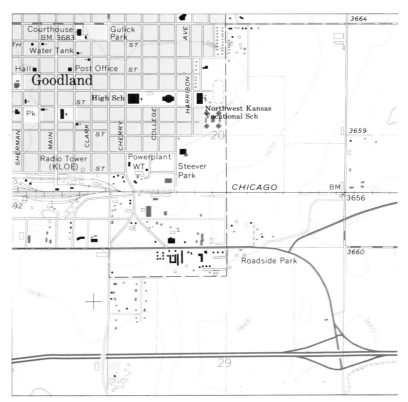

Using the information on the high-altitude photograph, cartographers made this detailed map of Goodland, Kansas.

make it necessary to update maps. In this way, technology provides mapmakers with the latest, most accurate information about the world.

Cartographers also make use of pictures taken by cameras mounted in aircraft. Very detailed maps can be produced from these high-altitude photographs, because all the roads and other features can be seen.

Because of advances in satellite technology and high-altitude photography, more details about the earth are constantly being discovered.

Geographic Features

The study of geography is the study of the people and the land, and any feature found on the surface of the earth can be called a geographic feature. Geographic features are either natural or human-made. They are a result of natural or human activity.

About 5,000 million years ago, our planet came into existence. Millions of years passed, air and water developed, and the shaping of the earth's crust began. Continents collided, thrusting up mountains. Erupting volcanoes created islands. Glaciers passed over the land, depositing rocks and soil and leaving lakes in their wake. Water, wind, and sand cut away at rock.

Humans shaped the land in a different way. They cut down trees to plant crops for food. They blocked the rivers with dams and built reservoirs to bring water to dry land. Mountains are rugged and difficult to farm, so people settled mostly in the valleys and on the plains, where the soil was rich and easy to cultivate. They built cities along coastlines and rivers, because transportation routes were available there. Soon developments were found even in the deserts, where irrigation gave life to the dry land.

This drawing shows some of the different kinds of geographic features on the surface of the earth. It is easy to see the difference between the human-made and natural features. Humans mark the land with bold, even shapes, such as squares and triangles. Nature, however, is not so uniform, and mountains and rivers often cut a jagged line across the earth.

The word list at the right defines some of these land and water features. The pages that follow show pictures of geographic features taken from satellites and aircraft. These pictures, called satellite images and high-altitude photographs, show what the land looks like from above. Satellite images and high-altitude photographs give cartographers the information they need to create maps.

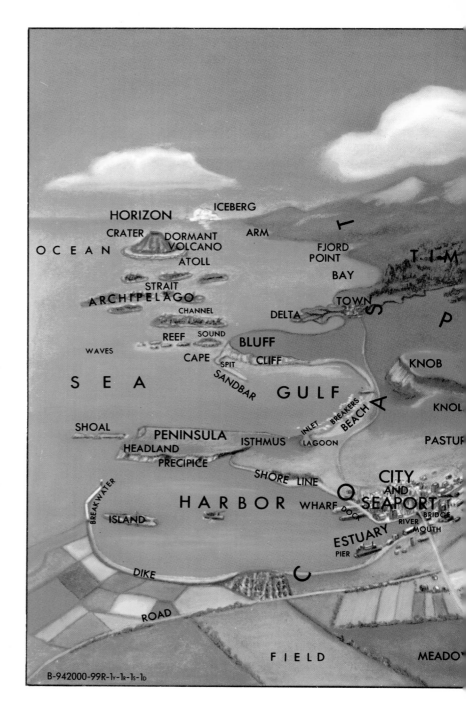

B-942000-99R-1v-1R-1s-1D

archipelago — A group of islands.

bay — Part of a lake or sea that is partly surrounded by the shore land.

canyon — A deep, narrow valley having high, steep sides or cliffs.

cape — A narrow part of land that sticks out into the water along a shore.

coast — Land along the sea.

delta — Land made by soil that drops from a river at its mouth, the place where it meets a larger body of water.

desert — A large land area in which there is little or no rainfall. Few plants can grow on this dry land.

divide — The high land that separates two river basins. A river drains the water from land, and that land is its basin.

fjord — A deep, narrow inlet of the sea, between high, steep cliffs.

forest — A large area of land where many trees grow.

gulf — A large area of the ocean or sea that lies within a curved coastline.

harbor — A sheltered body of water where ships anchor and are safe from the winds and waves of storms at sea.

hill — A small area of land that is higher than the land around it.

inlet — A small strip of water that

reaches from a sea or lake into the shore land.

island — Land that is surrounded by water and smaller than a continent.

isthmus — A narrow piece of land that joins two larger bodies of land.

lagoon — A pool of shallow water linked to the sea by an inlet.

lake — A body of water, usually fresh water, that is surrounded by land.

mountain — Land that rises very high, much higher than the land at its base. Mountains are much higher than hills.

mountain range — A row of mountains that are joined together. A mountain range makes a giant natural wall.

oasis — A place in a desert where people can get water. Water in an oasis comes from underground springs or from irrigation.

peninsula — A land area with a narrow link to a larger land area. It is almost surrounded by water.

plain — A large, flat land area.

plateau — A large land area that is high and generally very flat.

river — A large, moving body of fresh water that starts at a source in higher land. It drains the water from an area called its basin. The river moves from higher to lower land, and it carries the water to its mouth, where it ends. That mouth is at a lake, ocean, sea, or at another river.

sea — A large body of salt water nearly or partly surrounded by land. A sea is much smaller than an ocean.

sound — A long and wide body of water. A sound connects two larger bodies of water or separates an island from a larger body of land.

strait — A passageway of water that connects two large bodies of water.

tributary — A stream or small river that flows into another river or stream.

valley — The lower land between hills or mountains.

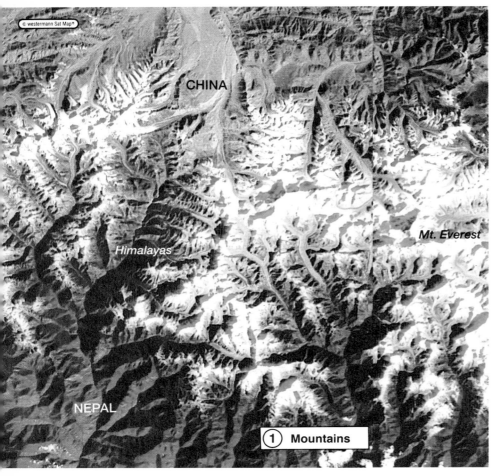

© westermann Sat Map*

CHINA

Himalayas

Mt. Everest

NEPAL

① Mountains

Mountains

High mountains arose millions of years ago, created by great collisions between the earth's "plates." Despite its appearance, the earth's crust, or outer layer, is actually made up of huge slow-moving plates. These plates are like rafts floating on the earth's mantle, the layer of the earth below the crust. Mountains are formed when these gigantic plates collide, thrusting one part of the earth high above the other.

One of the world's most rugged mountain systems is the Himalayas ①. Mount Everest, in the Himalayas, is the highest mountain in the world, rising to a height of 29,028 feet (8,848 meters).

Canyons

Canyons are deep, narrow valleys with steep sides. Most canyons were formed by streams or rivers that cut into rock. Water following the same path over a period of many years has the power to erode the land, carving a canyon in the earth's surface.

The Grand Canyon ② in Arizona is the largest canyon in the world and is

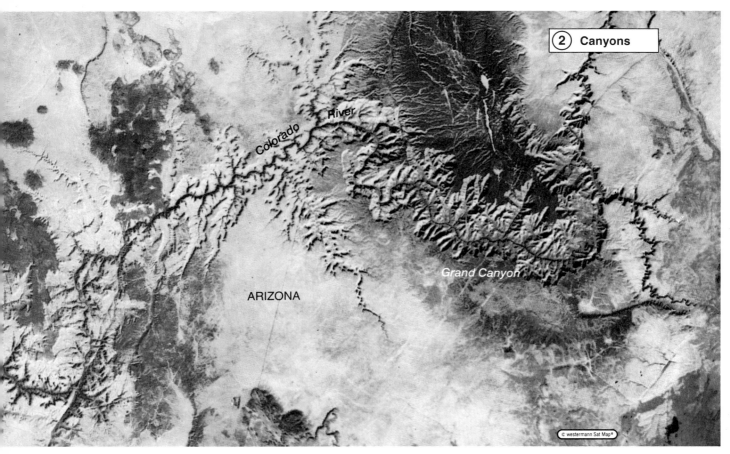

② Canyons

Colorado River

ARIZONA

Grand Canyon

© westermann Sat Map*

an example of how canyons form. Over a period of 10 million years, the Colorado River slowly cut into the earth's surface as it traveled to the sea. As the land was cut away, the canyon walls showed the different layers of colored rock that make up the earth. In the satellite image you can see the canyon and its river winding across the land. The dark brown and olive green areas are forests.

Volcanoes

The earth consists of three layers: an outer crust, a middle rock mantle, and an inner core. A volcano erupts when hot, molten rock, or magma, rises from the earth's mantle to its surface. Here it spews forth as lava. There are two kinds of volcanoes, shield volcanoes and cone-shaped volcanoes.

A shield volcano, or lava plateau, is formed when magma finds its way to the earth's surface through fissures, or openings in the earth's crust. The lava flows out gently to form these slightly arched volcanoes.

Cone-shaped volcanoes are formed by magma that contains water and gases. With explosive force, the magma erupts through central open-

ings in the earth, shooting gas, ash, and lava into the air. In time, the layers of lava and ash form the cone shape of the volcano.

Mount Saint Helens ③ is a cone-shaped volcano in western Washington State. It erupted with a fiery blast on May 18, 1980. The satellite image shows gray blue lava flows from the volcano that have covered forested land.

Deserts

Deserts are dry lands with low rainfall and sparse plant and animal life. Not all deserts are hot, sandy, and sunny. Deserts can also be cold, rocky, or snow and ice covered. In a polar desert, cold air keeps moisture from forming.

In some deserts, months or even years may pass with no rain. Then the sky darkens, and the rain comes in a short, violent storm.

The Makrān coastal region ④, which extends from Iran to Pakistan, is a desert off the Arabian Sea. The satellite image shows a dust storm in the desert. Dust clouds, heading out over the sea, appear along the lower edge of the picture.

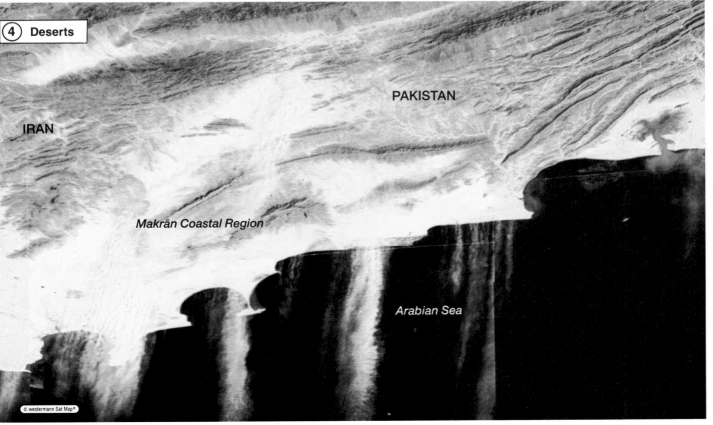

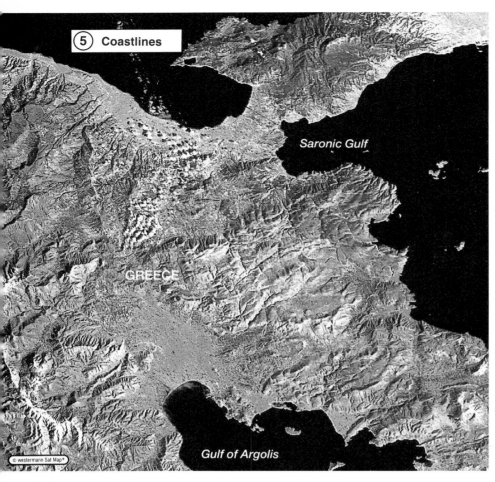

⑤ Coastlines

Saronic Gulf

GREECE

Gulf of Argolis

© westermann Sat Map®

Coastlines

The land along the sea is called the coast, and the coastline is the boundary between land and water. This boundary is always changing. Some changes occur slowly as the water carves out the land and fills in bays. Other changes occur daily. These are the tides that pull in and out, sifting and moving sand and sediment.

The satellite image of the Gulf of Argolis and the Saronic Gulf in Greece ⑤ shows the jagged line where the water meets the land.

Deltas

A delta is land that forms at a river's mouth, the place where the river meets a larger body of water. Here, the river slows down, and the clay, silt, sand, and gravel it has picked up on its journey drops to the bottom. In time, these deposits rise above the water ·to form a delta.

The Mississippi River ⑥ forms a delta where it meets the ocean near New Orleans. In the picture, the lighter blue around the river's mouth shows deposits that are slowly extending the delta into the Gulf of Mexico.

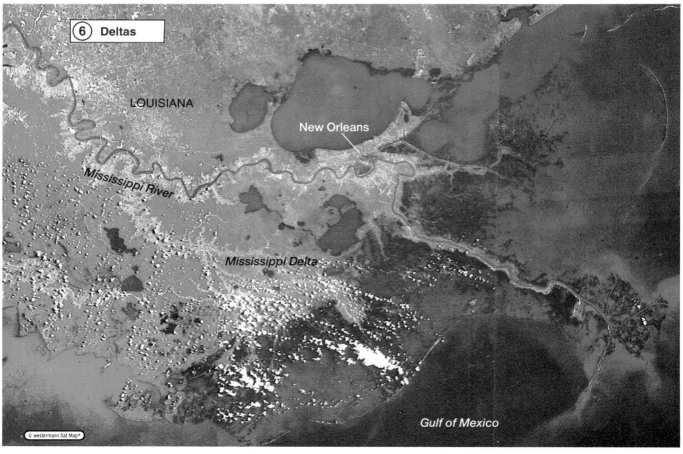

⑥ Deltas

LOUISIANA

New Orleans

Mississippi River

Mississippi Delta

Gulf of Mexico

© westermann Sat Map®

Islands

An island is a body of land that is smaller than a continent and completely surrounded by water. Islands are formed in different ways. Sometimes water crosses a peninsula or continent, cutting off a section of land as an island. Some islands are volcanoes or mountains resting on the ocean floor and extending above the water. Cays are low islands built from coral, sand, and algae reefs.

The Berry Islands ⑦ in the Bahamas are cays built upon a huge underwater limestone base. The green areas on satellite image are the cays, and the blue shows the reef that lies under the water.

Glaciers

A glacier is a slow-moving mass of ice found in high mountains and polar regions. Glaciers are formed when snow builds up year after year. The weight of the snow compacts it into glacial ice. As snow continues to fall and ice continues to form faster than it can melt, the glacier grows.

Many glaciers move only a fraction of an inch per day, and others move several feet. Some have moved up to 330 feet (101 meters) in a single day.

Glaciers are found in the St. Elias Mountains ⑧, which extend from Alaska into Canada. The mountains' Malaspina Glacier is larger than the state of Rhode Island.

⑨ Cultivated Land

OKLAHOMA

Indus River

Thal Desert

PAKISTAN

⑩ Rivers and Reservoirs

Cultivated Land

Agriculture is the science of producing crops and livestock. It provides the food that sustains human life, and so can be considered the most important of all employments. Land that people have altered to produce crops and feed livestock is called cultivated land.

The cultivated land of western Oklahoma ⑨ is an example of agriculture in the United States. Rectangular fields are bordered by country roads and highways. Tan areas in the image show cropland planted with wheat, which has just been harvested. Green areas are meadows and pastures used for livestock. The darker green sections are forests.

Rivers and Reservoirs

Water is essential for life, but water is not distributed evenly on the earth. Sometimes people shift water from lakes and rivers to dry land in order to help crops grow. This is called irrigation. Windmills, sprinklers, dams, reservoirs, and canals are some of the methods used for irrigation. People also use dams and reservoirs to block rivers and to obtain water for their daily use.

The Indus River ⑩ in Pakistan brings life to the surrounding land. In certain places dams block the river to control its flow. Reservoirs store water for irrigation and other purposes. And canals direct water away from the main

path of the river to bring water to the dry lands.

Cities

In settling the land, people were influenced by geographic factors. Some areas were too dry or too wet, subject to droughts or floods. Other places were hard to get to, blocked by mountains or far from the rivers used for transportation. So people settled in valleys, near mineral resources, and on fertile plains. They built their homes close to rivers and along harbors and bays. As time went on, more people were drawn to these population centers, looking for work and an easier life than farming could provide. Goods

(11) Cities

Washington, D.C.

White House

Capitol

Anacostia River

Potomac River

© westermann Sat Map®

were shipped in and out of busy ports, mineral deposits fueled growing industry, and railroads, highways, and air routes connected the important cities.

Because of their large populations and the effects of years of industry, cities today are facing many problems. However, they continue to play important roles as capitals of nations and centers of industry and technology.

The nation's capital, Washington, D.C., (11) is situated on a triangle of land formed by the Potomac and Anacostia rivers. Washington is part of an "urban corridor," a heavily populated area that extends all the way north to Boston, Massachusetts.

Cairo (12) is the capital of Egypt. It is situated where the Nile River broadens into the fertile Nile Delta. Transportation here is limited by the desert, and so all traffic and trade must pass through Cairo on its way north or south. Thus Cairo plays an important role in the economy and military strategy of the Middle East.

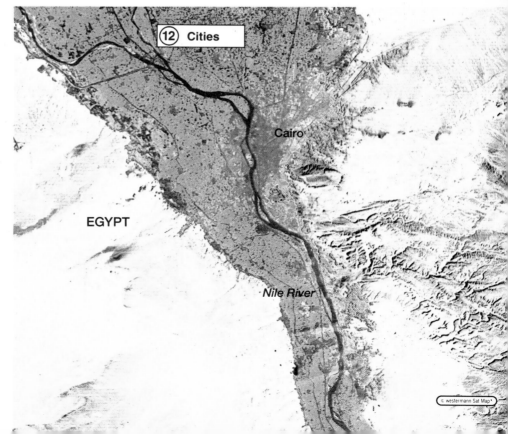

(12) Cities

Cairo

EGYPT

Nile River

© westermann Sat Map®

Using the Atlas

An atlas is a guide to the world that can be used in many ways. You can look up places in the news and learn about the world. If you're interested in history, you can use an atlas to find famous towns and battle sites. You can even use an atlas to find the names of places in movies or to look up the lake you swam in last summer. But to discover the world with your atlas, you must be able to do five things:

1. Measure distances using a map scale
2. Use directions and latitude and longitude
3. Find places on the maps using letter-number keys
4. Use different kinds of maps
5. Use map symbols and legends

Measuring Distances

To understand a map, you must know its scale, or how large an area of the earth it shows. There are different types of map scales, but the bar scale is the easiest to use for determining distance.

For example, to find the distance between Bergen and Oslo in Norway, first you will find out how far Bergen is from Oslo on the map. Then by using a bar scale, you will learn what this means in actual distance on the earth.

1. Find Bergen and Oslo on the map in Figure 1.
2. Lay a slip of paper on the map so that its edge touches the two

cities. Move the paper so that one corner touches Bergen.
3. Mark the paper where it touches Oslo. The distance from the corner of this paper to the mark shows how far Oslo is from Bergen on the map.

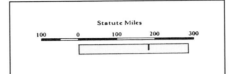

Figure 2

4. The numbers in the map scale in Figure 2 show statute miles, or miles on the earth. Line up the edge of the paper along the map scale, putting the corner at 0.
5. Find the mark on the paper. The mark shows that Bergen is about 200 miles away from Oslo.

Using Directions and Latitude and Longitude

Most of the maps in this atlas are drawn so that north is at the top of the page, south is at the bottom, west is at the left, and east is at the right.

Many of the maps also have lines drawn across them—lines of latitude and longitude. These are lines drawn on a map or globe to make it easier to tell directions and to find places.

Lines of latitude are also called parallels of latitude. As shown in Figure 3, parallels run east and west, and they are numbered with degrees, which measure distance. One degree of latitude is about seventy miles (112.65 kilometers) long.

Latitude is measured as degrees north (N) or degrees south (S) of the equator. The equator was chosen as the dividing point because it marks the middle of the earth. It is at 0° latitude. The place farthest north on earth is the North Pole. It is

located 90° north of the equator, or, simply, at 90° N. The South Pole is the earth's southernmost point, at 90° S.

You can use parallels of latitude to tell how far north or south a place is. For example, the map in Figure 1 shows that Bergen is north of the 60° parallel of latitude and Stockholm is south of it. So Bergen is farther north than Stockholm.

Lines of longitude are also called meridians. Figure 3 shows that meridians run north and south between the two poles. Like parallels, they are numbered with degrees.

But unlike parallels of latitude, meridians have no natural dividing line at which their numbering can begin. In the 1880s, an international conference solved this problem by

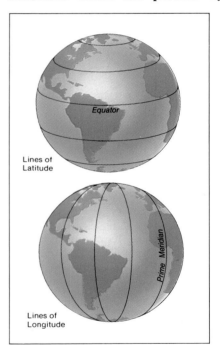

Figure 3

selecting Greenwich, England, near London, to be the prime meridian, or 0° longitude. So, meridians measure how far east (E) or west (W) of Greenwich, England, a place is.

You can use the map in Figure 1 to find out which city is farther east, Bergen or Stockholm. Bergen is about 5° east of the prime meridian, or 5° E. Stockholm is about 20° E. This means that Stockholm is farther east than Bergen.

The east-west parallels and north-south meridians form a grid on a globe or map. You can find any place in the world by using latitude and longitude.

Figure 1

Finding Places

One of the most important things an atlas can do is tell you the location of a place—where it is. You may want to look up the city where a pen pal lives or find a town you're interested in visiting. To help you find places quickly and easily on a map, most atlases include an index of place-names with letter-number keys.

If you were studying South America, and read about Santiago, a city in Chile, here's how you would find it on a map:

1. Look up the city's name, Santiago, in the alphabetical index at the back of the atlas. (See Figure 4.) The number 88 is the page that the map is on. The letter-number key C2 is the guide to finding Santiago on the map on page 88.
2. Turn to the map of southern South America on page 88.
3. Find the letters **A** through **G** along the left-hand side of the map and the numbers **2** through **5** along the top edge of the map. These black letters and numbers are centered between the parallels of latitude and meridians of longitude.

Figure 4

4. To find Santiago, use the letter-number key C2. Place your left index finger on C and your right index finger on 2. Move your left finger across the map and your right finger down the map, staying within the latitude and longitude grid lines on either side. Your fingers will meet in the box in which Santiago is located. (See Figure 5.)

You can use this method to find any place listed in the index of this atlas.

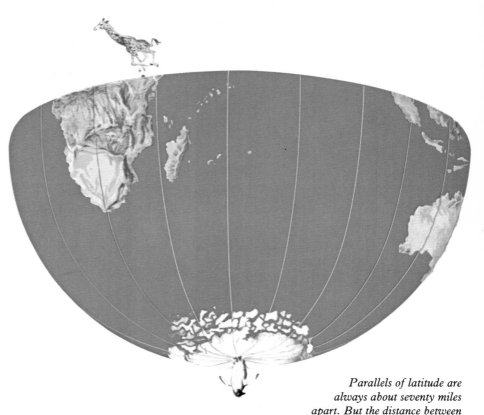

Parallels of latitude are always about seventy miles apart. But the distance between meridians shrinks near the North and South poles. At the equator, a giraffe would have to run seventy miles (112.65 kilometers) to cover one degree of longitude. Near the South Pole, a penguin could merely wiggle a toe over the ice and cross a meridian.

Figure 5

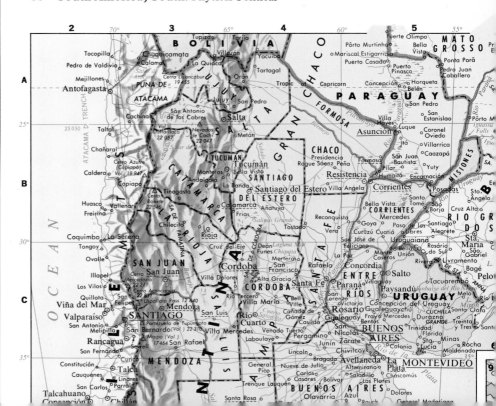

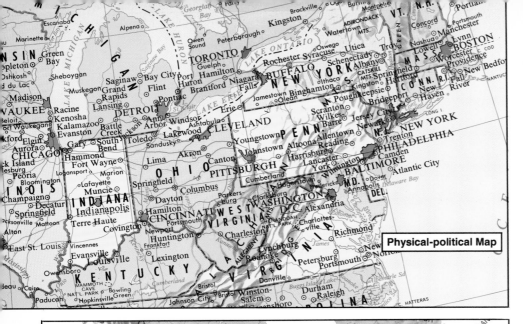

Physical-political Map

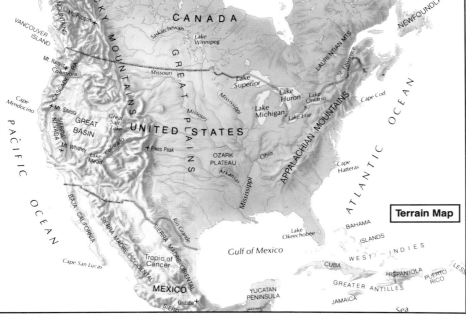

Terrain Map

Thematic Map

Using Different Kinds of Maps

There are different kinds of maps, and each is especially suited for a certain topic. In this atlas, you'll find physical-political maps, physical maps, political maps, and thematic maps.

When people think of maps, they usually think of physical-political maps. The purpose of a physical-political map is to show the world's physical features and political units. Physical features include oceans, lakes, rivers, mountains, and other natural parts of the earth. Political units are states and countries and all the places they contain. These are human-made features.

Sometimes, the information on a physical-political map is separated to make two maps: a physical map, showing only natural features, and a political map, showing only human-made features.

The physical maps in this atlas are called terrain maps. The terrain maps use shaded relief to show the shape of the earth's surface. Shaded relief is a three-dimensional drawing of mountains and valleys on a map. The political maps in this atlas show countries, major cities, roads, and railroads.

A thematic map tells the story of a special topic, such as rainfall, population, trade, mineral resources, or any special aspect of the physical (natural) or political (human-made) environment. There are two main types of thematic maps in this atlas: environ-

PHYSICAL-POLITICAL MAP (top)
Physical-political maps are sometimes called general reference maps because they give general information about the world's natural and human-made features. You can use physical-political maps to find cities and countries, to measure distances, or to look up mountains, lakes, and other physical features.

TERRAIN MAP (center)
A physical, or terrain, map shows only natural features. On this map of the United States, the shaded relief indicates that the West is marked with high mountains, the central United States is mainly a plain, and the East consists of highlands and low mountains.

THEMATIC MAP (bottom)
Using a thematic map is much like looking at a picture. This thematic map of the United States can tell you what type of wildlife is found in your part of the country.

ment maps and animal maps. The environment maps show how people use the land. The animal maps show the kinds of wildlife found on each continent.

Using Map Symbols and Legends

A symbol is something that stands for something else. In a way, a whole map is a symbol, because it represents the world or a part of it.

All the world's features—such as cities, rivers, and lakes—are represented with symbols on maps. Map symbols may be points, lines, or areas.

Point symbols are usually dots or stars. For example, the symbol for a city might be a dot, and the symbol for a state capital might be a star.

Line symbols are used for roads, rivers, or railroads. Often, rivers are shown with blue lines, and roads with black.

Area symbols show states, forests, deserts, or anything that covers a large area. On a map of the United States, for example, each state may be shown in a different color so that you can see where one state ends and the next state begins. Large areas of forest might be shown in green, and deserts could be a

sand color. These different colors are area symbols.

A map legend explains the symbols used on the map. It is called a legend because it tells the story of the map. It is sometimes called a map key, because it unlocks the meaning of the map's symbols.

The environment map legend below divides the environment into ten major categories. If the area mapped has a city character with streets, factories, and buildings, it is shown as urban. If most of the area is farmland with crops, it falls into the cropland category. This legend should be used when reading the environment maps in the book.

The physical-political map legend at the right divides the earth's geographic features into three major classes: cultural, land, and water features. Cultural features are human-made and include cities, roads, railroads, and boundaries. Land features are mountain peaks, mountain passes, and spot heights. (Spot heights tell the elevation of certain places on a mountain.) Water features are rivers, lakes, swamps, and any body of water. This legend should be used when working with the physical-political maps in the book.

PHYSICAL-POLITICAL MAP LEGEND

CULTURAL FEATURES

Political Boundaries
- ——— International
- ——— Intercolonial
- ——— Secondary: State, Provincial, etc.

Cities, Towns and Villages
(Except for scales of 1:20,000,000 or smaller)
- PARIS — 1,000,000 and over
- Ufa — 500,000 to 1,000,000
- Győr — 50,000 to 500,000
- Agadir — 25,000 to 50,000
- Moreno — 0 to 25,000
- TŌKYŌ — National Capitals
- Boise — Secondary Capitals

Transportation
- ——— Railroads
- --------- Railroad Ferries
- ········· Caravan Routes

Other Cultural Features
- Dams
- Pipelines
- ▲ Pyramids
- ∴ Ruins

LAND FEATURES
- △ Peaks, Spot Heights
- = Passes

WATER FEATURES

Lakes and Reservoirs
- Fresh Water
- Fresh Water: Intermittent
- Salt Water
- Salt Water: Intermittent

Other Water Features
- Swamps
- Glaciers
- Rivers
- Canals
- Aqueduct — Aqueducts
- Ship Channels
- Falls
- Rapids
- Springs
- Water Depths
- Sand Bars
- Reefs

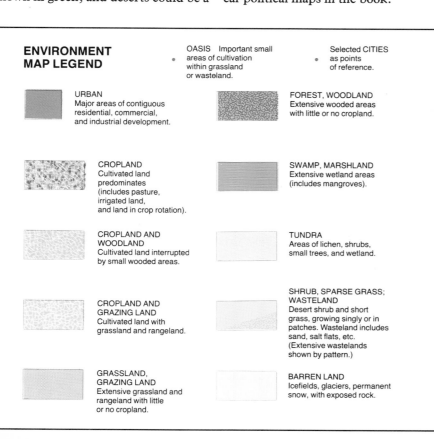

ENVIRONMENT MAP LEGEND

OASIS Important small areas of cultivation within grassland or wasteland.

Selected CITIES as points of reference.

URBAN
Major areas of contiguous residential, commercial, and industrial development.

FOREST, WOODLAND
Extensive wooded areas with little or no cropland.

CROPLAND
Cultivated land predominates (includes pasture, irrigated land, and land in crop rotation).

SWAMP, MARSHLAND
Extensive wetland areas (includes mangroves).

CROPLAND AND WOODLAND
Cultivated land interrupted by small wooded areas.

TUNDRA
Areas of lichen, shrubs, small trees, and wetland.

CROPLAND AND GRAZING LAND
Cultivated land with grassland and rangeland.

SHRUB, SPARSE GRASS; WASTELAND
Desert shrub and short grass, growing singly or in patches. Wasteland includes sand, salt flats, etc. (Extensive wastelands shown by pattern.)

GRASSLAND, GRAZING LAND
Extensive grassland and rangeland with little or no cropland.

BARREN LAND
Icefields, glaciers, permanent snow, with exposed rock.

Europe/Terrain

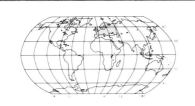

Europe Facts

Sixth largest continent
Second in population: 664,600,000
63 cities over 1 million population
Highest mountain: Elbrus, 18,510 feet
    (5,642 meters)
Most densely populated continent: 173 people
    per square mile (67 people per square
    kilometer)

Many parts of Europe lie under the shadows of towering mountains. The most splendid of these peaks are the Alps. These shining pyramids of snow and stone are found in Switzerland, southeastern France, Austria, southern Germany, northern Italy, and northern Yugoslavia. The Alps make these countries a sightseer's paradise and a skier's adventureland.

Three major mountain systems flow out of the central mass of the Alps like tails from a kite. One of these tails, the Apennines, reaches south into the boot of Italy. Another, the Dinaric Alps, makes a jagged trail through Yugoslavia and Albania into Greece. The third, the Carpathians, forms a graceful half-moon through Czechoslovakia and Romania.

Also reaching out from the Alps are many hills and plateaus. Nearly all of southern and central France is a wide upland, the Massif Central, that has been cut by rivers into hills. More hills ruffle parts of northern France and eastern Belgium—they are called the Ardennes Mountains, site of many fierce battles throughout history. Similar low hills and plateaus lie across southern Germany, in parts of Czechoslovakia, and in Austria.

Across the English Channel, Great Britain has a bumpy backbone known as the Pennine Chain of mountains. North of them are the famed Scottish Highlands, where long hills covered with heather roll like frozen ocean waves across the countryside.

Northern mainland Europe is

© 1979 Rand McNally & Co.

marked by mountains of another kind. The uplands of Norway and Sweden are bleak and barren, especially as they approach the white magnificence of the Arctic Circle. Huge glaciers once rumbled over the landscape, clawing deep grooves into the mountains. These grooves, flooded by the ocean, have become long waterways called fjords. The fjords attract many tourists because of their awesome beauty.

Far to the east the Soviet Union's Ural Mountains mark the division between Europe and Asia. Such a mountain chain in the middle of a thousand-mile flatland is most unusual. The Urals are very old—formed about 225 million years ago. In that time they have worn down more and more.

Today the tallest of the Urals stands only a little more than six thousand feet (1,828.2 meters) above sea level, quite low in comparison with other major mountains.

Some of the most famous rivers in the world flow from Europe's mountains. Perhaps the best known is the Rhine, which rises in Switzerland and flows north past grape-clothed bluffs in Germany and France where the castles of medieval barons still scowl down on the river. Far longer than the Rhine is the fabled Danube River. It rises in Germany and drifts lazily in a southeasterly direction through seven nations and three capital cities before emptying into the Black Sea.

The north-central part of the continent is made up of the Great Northern European Plain. The huge region's rich farmlands supply food for much of Europe, and its many ores help to make the Ruhr Valley on the Rhine a world center for heavy industry. Food and machinery move out to the rest of Europe on a network of rivers connected by canals. The canals were dug by hand long ago in spillways, the natural trenches that were formed by the melting of the glacier twenty-five thousand years ago.

The Great Northern European Plain stretches from western France to nearly a thousand miles (1,609.3 kilometers) beyond Moscow, where it is broken at last by the rounded Urals. Here bustling Europe ends amid the lonely sweep of the wind through mountain forests.

The Scottish Highlands are so rough and rugged that many people live instead on the lower coastal plains. Here the land is more easily farmed.

The coasts of Norway and Sweden were formed by glaciers pushing into the sea. When the ice melted, the sea filled the winding fingers, or fjords. Some fjords are nearly 4,000 feet (1,219.2 kilometers) deep.

Mykonos, at left, and the other Greek islands in the Aegean Sea are part of the Pindus Mountains of Greece. Millions of years ago the sea rose until only the tops of the mountains remained above the waters.

Urban

Cropland

Cropland & Woodland

Cropland & Grazing Land

Grassland, Grazing Land

Forest, Woodland

Swamp, Marshland

Tundra

Shrub, Sparse Grass,
Wasteland (pattern)

Barren Land

Oasis

Reykjavik

Narvik

Trondheim

Une

Gulf of Bothnia

Bergen

Oslo

Helsinki   ST.
PETERSBUR

Tallinn

Stockholm

Göteborg

ATLANTIC

Glasgow

Belfast

MANCHESTER

Dublin

Copenhagen

Baltic Sea

Riga

Kaliningrad

Vilnius

OCEAN

Hamburg

Amsterdam

Elbe

BERLIN

Minsk

London

Antwerp

Essen

Oder

Warsaw

P

Leipzig

Frankfurt

North
Sea

Brest

PARIS   Seine

Strasbourg

Prague

Kraków

L'vov

Loire

Danube

C A R P A

Bay of Biscay

Munich

VIENNA

Rhône

Zürich

BUDAPEST

La Coruña

Bordeaux

Gironne

Lyon

Tisza

Bilbao

Rhône

MILAN

Zagreb

Belgrade

Douro

P Y R E N E E S

Venice

Sava

Bucharest

MADRID

Ebro

Genoa

Adriatic

Danube

Lisbon

BARCELONA

Marseille

CORSICA

ROME

Sea

Sofia

Sevilla

Tirane

Tanger

ISLAS BALEARES

SARDINIA

Naples

Aegean
Sea

Algiers

Tyrrhenian Sea

Palermo

Athens

Oran

M e d i t e r r a n e a n

Casablanca   ATLAS   MOUNTAINS

Tunis

SICILY

MALTA

S e a

CRETE

Longitude West of Greenwich   0°   Longitude East of Greenwich

Scale   1:16,500,000 one inch to 260 miles. Conic Projection

0   50   100   200   300   400   500 Miles
0   100   200   400   600   800 Kilometers

Nar'yan-Mar

Pechora

Ob'

Novosibirsk

Irtysh

te Sea

Archangelsk

Omsk

URALS

YEKATERINBURG

Karaganda

Perm'

Kirov

Vologda

Kama

Ufa

Volga

Magnitogorsk

Kazan'

Balkhash

Nizhniy
Novgorod

Orsk

Samara

MOSCOW

Volga

Kzyl-Orda

Tula

Syr-Dar'ya

Saratov

Ural

PESKI
KYZYLKUM

DEPRESSION

Khar'kov

CASPIAN

Aral'skoye
More
(Aral Sea)

Amu Dar'ya

VOLGOGRAD

Don

Volga

Astrakhan'

Dnepropetrovsk

Donetsk

MANYCH

DEPRESSION

PESKI KARAKUMY

Dnepr

Krasnodar

Odessa

Ashkhabad

C a s p i a n

CAUCASUS MTS.

BAKU

TBILISI

S e a

B l a c k   S e a

Yerevan

ANBUL

ELBURZ MTS.

Ankara

TEHRAN

DASHT-E-KAVIR

ZAGROS

Kerman

Tigris

MOUNTAINS

Euphrates

Baghdad

Nicosia

CYPRUS

Beirut

Abadan

Europe/Animals

Skua

Herring

Barnacle Goose

Reindeer

Grey Seal

Wolverine

Lemming

Hare

Basking Shark

Red Deer

Otter

Black Grouse

Badger

Pheasant

Hedgehog

Rabbit

Fox

Atlantic Salmon

Moorhen

Red-legged Partridge

Chamois

Stork

Marmot

Squirrel

Great Bustard

Barbary Ape

Sole

Ferruginous Duck

Spanish Mackerel

Hoopoe

Raven

Whimbrel

Brown Bear

Pine Marten

Wild Boar

Wolf

Griffon
Vulture

Roe Deer

Lesser
Spotted Eagle

Tur

Octopus

Conger Eel

Most of the vast, animal-filled forests that once covered much of Europe were cut down long ago to make room for farms, cities, and towns. Many of Europe's animals were hunted for centuries, until they were wiped out. But in a few wild places still left—national parks, game preserves, and a few out-of-the-way places—some of the animals that once abounded in Europe can still be found.

A few of the shaggy, tusked boars that were the favorite game animal of medieval nobles still root in the underbrush of small forests in central Europe. Packs of wolves still howl in some places, and in the northern Soviet Union brown bears still lumber about. In the north of Sweden, Norway, Finland, and the western Soviet Union reindeer are herded like cattle by people of the northland, the Lapps.

In the Pyrenees Mountains between France and Spain lives the Pyrenean ibex, a mountain goat with curled horns. Another kind of mountain goat, the chamois, is found in the Alps.

Europe also has numerous small animals. Foxes, badgers, moles, rabbits, and squirrels are found in many places. Little, plump lemmings abound in the mountains of Norway and Sweden. The hedgehog is common in northern Europe and especially well-known in England. It has short, sharp "spikes" all over its back, like the quills of a porcupine only much thicker.

Small, striped wildcats prowl in parts of Yugoslavia and Bulgaria, and a rather large wildcat, the Spanish lynx, lives in Spain. It is three feet (0.91 meter) long with pointed ears and thick whiskers—a fast, fierce hunter.

Sparrows, thrushes, finches, nightingales, and ravens are found throughout central Europe. So are large birds of prey such as falcons and eagles. During the summer the big white stork is a common sight in cities of the Netherlands, Belgium, and Germany, where it nests on the chimneys of houses.

Various kinds of lizards and snakes, tortoises and turtles, frogs, toads, and salamanders are found in woodlands and meadows throughout Europe. Trout, salmon, and other fish swim in clear streams above the polluted areas. Many of the animal species found in Europe are also found on the North American continent.

In a protected forest of Poland about 1,600 wisents, the bisons of prehistoric Europe, live as they did many thousands of years ago—feeding in grassy clearings. Full grown, the animals stand six feet (1.82 meters) high at the shoulder.

Europe/Countries and Cities

In some ways Europe looks more like a jigsaw puzzle than a reasonable grouping of thirty-three nations. The boundaries of those countries—from the huge Soviet Union to tiny Luxembourg—were agreed upon only after much haggling through the centuries. In recent times, World Wars I and II caused boundary changes, and several new nations were formed as well.

The borders of most countries stop at mountains, rivers, or seas. When the first tribes migrated into an area, they usually chose a homeland that had some natural barrier where their warriors could defend them from attack. Today, many countries still are edged by such natural borders.

Cities tell us much about peoples of the past. Rome and Athens were known thousands of years ago, and the Roman Forum and Colosseum and the Acropolis and statues of Athens hint at life in ancient times. Paris dates back more than two thousand years. It was founded around 52 B.C. by Roman

soldiers. Trondheim, in Norway, had its beginning around A.D. 998. Today it is the third largest city in Norway and an important export center. Clues in these and other cities hint at governments, religions, and pastimes of the people who once lived there.

The European continent averages 173 persons per square mile. Some of its countries, especially in the west, are among the most densely packed in the world. The Netherlands has 892 persons per square mile. But it is doing something few other countries are able to do—it is growing by reclaiming land from the sea.

Something a traveler moving through Europe notices is its many languages. Of the several dozen spoken, nearly all fall into three main groups.

The French, Italians, Spanish, Portuguese, and Romanians cannot understand one another. Nevertheless, all of their languages are based on the ancient Latin spoken by the Romans who once conquered those lands. These are the "Romance" languages.

The people of Germany, the Netherlands, England, Denmark, Sweden, and Norway speak six separate languages. Yet these, too, have their roots

About 2,300 years ago, Rome was the heart of Europe. Still standing are parts of the Roman Forum, which was both a marketplace and a meeting place for Roman citizens. The great pillars of the Forum buildings stood for the strength of the Roman Empire, which ruled over 50 million people on three continents.

in a single language—the German of the tribes which occupied those areas in ages past.

To the east, the peoples of Poland, Czechoslovakia, Yugoslavia, Bulgaria, and Russia all speak languages based on the Slavic language of tribes that once lived there.

You might ask why an Italian doesn't understand a Spaniard, since their languages are alike. Or why the Germanic-speaking Dane doesn't understand the Germanic-speaking Briton. The answer lies in terrain, distance, and culture. Peoples of neighboring lands often were cut off from each other by natural barriers, or were separated by too many miles to meet often and talk. The Pyrenees closed Spain from France. A branch of the Alps shut off France from Italy. The North Sea separated the English from the Danes. And vast differences

in cultures—life-styles—divided the Slavic-speaking Poles and the Russians. Each nation developed—over long ages—different ways of speaking what were once the same languages. In time the German of Germany was slightly different from that of the Netherlands. Across the North Sea the English people developed a distinct language using many German words, but also including words from Latin. And in the north, the Danes, Swedes, and Norwegians all used their own versions of the ancient German.

Today European languages are called Romance, Germanic, and Slavic. Only three major European countries do not fall into these groupings: Finland, Hungary, and Greece.

Each of the thirty-three nations of Europe has its own kind of government and a way of life that is unique to itself.

40,000 SQ MI
AREA

0   100   200
Miles

Cities,
Towns,
and
Villages

0 to 25,000   100,000 to 250,000   1,000,000 and over

25,000 to 100,000   250,000 to 1,000,000   Major urbanized area

0 50 100   200   300   400   500 Miles
0   100   200   400   600   800 Kilometers

Scale 1:16,850,000 ; one inch to 265 miles. Conic Projection

Elevations and depressions are given in feet

ATLANTIC OCEAN

B

ARCTIC

ZEMLYA FRANTSA IOSIFA
(FRANZ JOSEF LAND)

SVALBARD
(SPITSBERGEN)
(Nor.)

BARENTS SEA

NOVAYA ZEMLYA

M. ZHELANIYA

KARSKOYE
(Kara Sea)

Matochkin Shar

BELYY

UNITED KINGDOM
Glasgow
Edinburgh
Aberdeen
Newcastle

NORTH SEA

NORWAY
SWEDEN
Bergen
Trondheim
Oslo
Göteborg
Norrköping

FINLAND
LAPLAND
Gulf of Bothnia
Luleå
Kemi

Arctic Circle

Hammerfest
Vardö
Nordkapp

Murmansk
Polyarnyy
KOL'SKIY
Kirovsk
(KOLA PEN.)
Kandalaksha

DENMARK
COPENHAGEN
Ålborg
Kiel
Malmö

GERMANY
HAMBURG
BERLIN
Poznań
Łódź

BALTIC SEA
STOCKHOLM
Turku
Helsinki
Vyborg

ESTONIA
Tallinn
Tartu
Pskov'

LATVIA
Riga

LITHUANIA
Kaunas
Vilnius

POLAND
WARSAW
Gdańsk
Kaliningrad
Brest

BYELORUSSIA
Minsk
Mogilev
Gomel'

WHITE SEA
Arkhangelsk
(Archangel)

Petrozavodsk
KARELIAN A.S.S.R.
Kem'

Onega

P-OV KANIN
Mezen'
Cheshskaya Guba

PECHORA BASIN
Nar'yan-Mar
Ust'-Tsil'ma
Pechora

KOMI A.S.S.R.
Syktyvkar
Ust'-Kulom

P-OV YAMAL
Khabarovo
VAYGACH
Kara
Novyy Port

Salekhard
Vorkuta
Khal'mer-Yu

ST. PETERSBURG
(Leningrad)
Tikhvin
Cherepovets
Vologda

MOSCOW
(Moskva)
Tver'
Yaroslavl'
Kostroma
Ivanovo
Vladimir
Serpukhov
Ryazan'
Kaluga

NIZHNIY NOVGOROD
Shuya
Murom
Arzamas

Kirov
Glazov
Perm'
Kungur
Krasnou...

UKRAINE
KIEV (Kiyev)
Zhitomir
Vinnitsa
Chernovtsy
L'vov
Berdichev
Kishinev
MOLDAVIA

KHARKOV
Poltava
Sumy
Kursk
Orël
Voronezh
Lipetsk
Tambov
Penza
Saratov

DNEPROPETROVSK
Krivoy Rog
Zaporozh'ye
DONETSK
Lugansk
Shakhty

Odessa
Nikolayev
Simferopol'
Sevastopol'
Kerch'
Krasnodar

BLACK SEA
Sochi
Novorossiysk
Maykop
Armavir
Stavropol'

CAUCASUS MTS.
Grozny
GEORGIA
Batumi
Tbilisi
ARMENIA
Yerevan
AZERBAIJAN
BAKU

CASPIAN SEA
Astrakhan
Gur'yev
CASPIAN DEPRESSION
Surface 92 feet below Sea Level

SAMARA
Buzuluk
Ul'yanovsk
Syzran'
Kazan'
Izhevsk

YEKATERINBURG
Nizhniy Tagil
Zlatoust
Chelyabinsk
Magnitogorsk
Sterlitamak
Ufa
Orenburg
Orsk
Aktyubinsk

WESTERN SIBERIAN LOWLAND
Khanty-Mansiysk
Surgut
Tyumen'
Tobol'sk
Tomsk
Narym

RUSSIAN

Kurgan
Petropavlovsk
Omsk
Tatarsk
Kuybyshev
Barnaul
NOVOSIBIRSK
Anzhero-Sudzhensk

KIRGHIZ STEPPE
KAZAKHSTAN
Ural'sk
Kustanay
Turgay
Tselinograd
(Akmolinsk)
Karaganda
Temir Tau
Semipalatinsk
Pavlodar
Rubtsovsk
Zyryanovsk

Aral'sk
ARAL'SKOYE MORE
(Aral Sea)
Novo-Kazalinsk
Kzyl-Orda

TURKESTAN
Chimkent
Dzhambul
Alma-Ata
KIRGHIZIA
Pishpek
Frunze

TASHKENT
UZBEKISTAN
Samarkand
Bukhara
Kokand
Andizhan
Fergana

TURKMENISTAN
Krasnovodsk
Ashkhabad
PESKI KARAKUMY (DESERT)
PESKI KYZYL KUM (DESERT)
Chardzhou
Mary

TAJIKISTAN
Dushanbe

TURKEY
Samsun
Trabzon
Erzurum
Kars

IRAQ
Baghdad
Kirkuk
Al Mawsil

IRAN
TEHRAN
Tabriz
Mashhad
ELBURZ MTS.
ZAGROS MTS.
DASHT-E KAVIR

TIEN SHAN
Kashgar
CHINA

Scale 1:21,500,000; one inch to 340 ...
Lambert's Azimuthal, Equal Area Pro...
Elevations and depressions are given...

Asia/Terrain

Asia covers more area than North America, Europe, and Australia combined. Great numbers of people struggle for a living in Asia—nearly two and a half billion, more people than live in all the rest of the world! Yet because Asia is so big, there are places where an eagle could fly for hours, even days, and never see a human being.

The empty, and nearly empty, parts of Asia take up more space than parts of the continent where people live. For example, the area of the Soviet Union known as Siberia reaches eastward from the Ural Mountains, where Asia begins, for more than three thousand long, lonely miles (4,827.9 kilometers) to the Pacific Ocean. It is a vast region of cold winds and frosty earth.

To the south of Siberia is an equally large, equally harsh region. A desert blots out most life across central Asia. This desert begins in the blowing sand dunes of Saudi Arabia, sweeps across much of Jordan, Iraq, and Iran, and continues through the southern Soviet Union. It blisters Mongolia, where it ends as the forbidding Gobi Desert.

The great Asian desert is bounded on the south by the highest mountain ranges in the world. Highest of all are the Himalayas. Mount Everest, in the Himalayas, reaches five and a half miles (8.85 kilometers) into air so thin that climbers must wear oxygen masks to stay alive.

South of the Himalayas lies a warm, wet triangle of land, the subcontinent of India. Some of the most important areas in India and Bangladesh are around the Ganges and Brahmaputra rivers. This is the agricultural core of the land. Jute, rice, wheat, and sugarcane are grown here.

Summer monsoons—rain-bearing winds—sweep across India from June to September. The monsoons blow from the southwest, across the Indian Ocean, picking up moisture and carrying rain to India and part of Pakistan. The monsoons make the difference between good and bad crops. Since the winds do not reach far into Pakistan, some of the people there must irrigate their land. They rely on water from the Indus River, which rises in Tibet north of the Himalayas and flows through Pakistan.

That part of Asia called the Far East includes three of the most heavily populated countries in the world: China, Japan, and Korea.

For thousands of years, China was cut off from other countries. Frigid Siberia and the bleak Gobi Desert separated China from Europe. The plateau of Tibet, three miles (4.82 kilometers) high, and the Himalayas beyond were a barrier between China and India. With the growth of seamanship in the West, China began to trade with other countries.

China's climate is cool in the north, warm and wet in the south. This makes a difference in the kind of food grown in the areas—wheat in the north, rice in the south.

China has three major rivers. In the north is the Hwang Ho (Yellow) River. The Yangtze is in the south, so is the Hsi. People have settled heavily along these rivers.

Japan was once cut off from its neighbors, too. The Pacific Ocean made trade difficult. China was more than 400 miles (643.72 kilometers) away and Korea was 100 miles (160.93 kilometers) away.

The four main Japanese islands are part of a chain of rather recently formed volcanic mountains. Much of the land is covered with volcanic ash and lava which once spouted from such mighty cones as Mount Fuji. Japan still feels the effects of its volcanic birth. The land somewhere in

Farmers grow rice on the hilly terrain of Nepal by planting their crops in terraced fields. Beyond loom the Himalayas, the highest mountains in the world.

Israel's Negev Desert blooms with the help of water pumped from the Sea of Galilee.

© 1979 Rand McNally & Co.

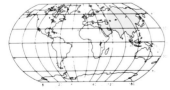

Asia Facts

Largest continent
First in population: 2,631,600,000
78 cities with over 1 million population
World's highest mountain: Everest, 29,028 feet
(8,847.73 meters)
World's largest "lake": Caspian Sea, 152,084
square miles (393,897.56 square kilometers)
World's lowest inland point: Dead Sea, 1,299
feet (395.93 meters) below sea level

Japan shakes with an earthquake on the average of four times a day.

South of China is the area known as Southeast Asia. It includes Indochina, the Malay Peninsula, and the islands of Indonesia. The region is a gigantic rain forest, and the air is steamy. There are a few fertile river valleys—the Mekong, which passes through nearly all of Indochina; the Menam in Thailand; and the Irrawaddy in Burma.

In Indonesia, near the equator, the climate becomes even hotter. These islands are part of a mountain chain which is mostly hidden under the sea. The dark trees, thick undergrowth, and looping vines of dripping rain forests cover all the islands except Java.

Asia is a vast continent. It has some of the world's highest mountains, longest rivers, largest deserts, and coldest and hottest climates.

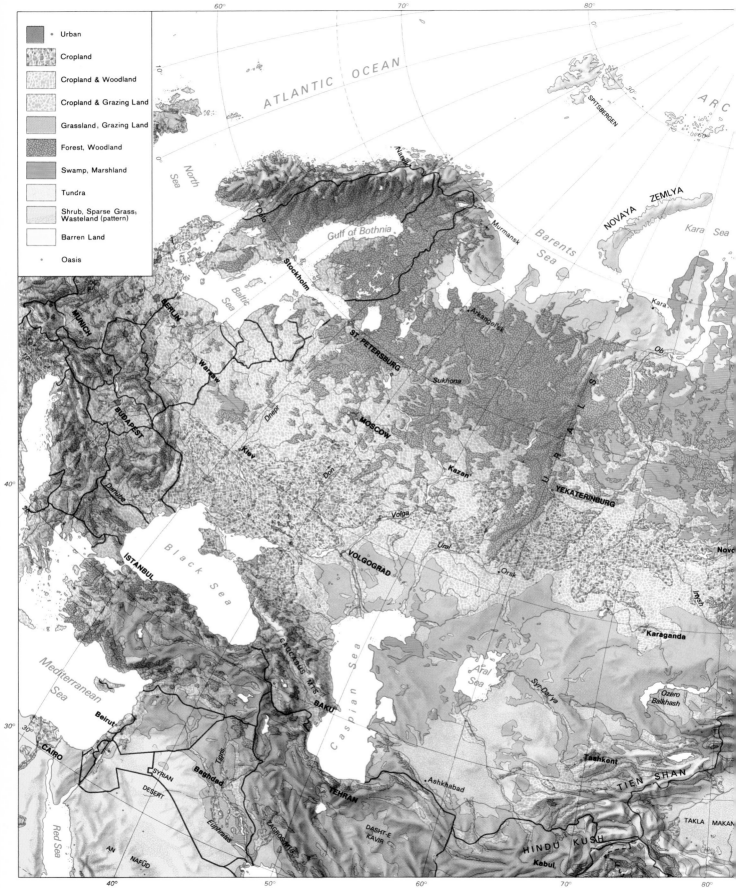

Urban
Cropland
Cropland & Woodland
Cropland & Grazing Land
Grassland, Grazing Land
Forest, Woodland
Swamp, Marshland
Tundra
Shrub, Sparse Grass,
Wasteland (pattern)
Barren Land
Oasis

Scale 1:24,800,000; one inch to 390 miles. Lambert Azimuthal Equal-Area Projection

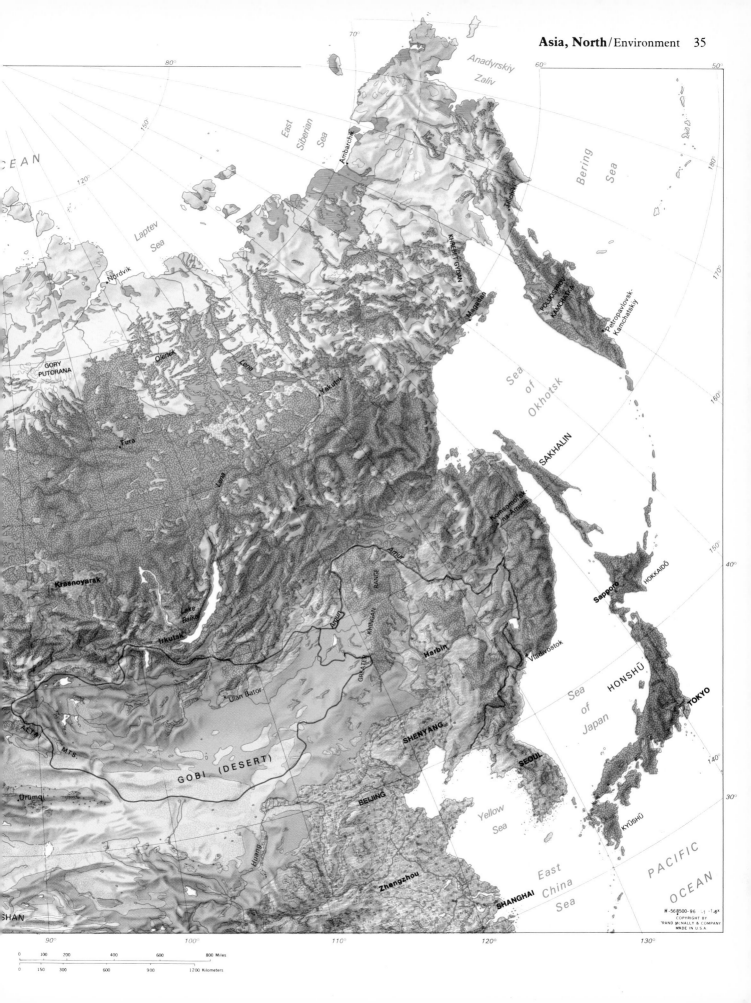

OCEAN

East Siberian Sea

Anadyrskiy Zaliv

70°

80°

60°

50°

150°

120°

180°

Laptev Sea

Ambarchik

Bering Sea

Iligino

170°

Nordvik

KHREBET GYDAN

POLUOSTROV KAMCHATKA

Petropavlovsk-Kamchatskiy

Olenek

Lena

Magadan

160°

GORY PUTORANA

Yakutsk

Sea of Okhotsk

Tura

SAKHALIN

Lena

Komsomolsk-na-Amure

150°

HOKKAIDŌ

40°

Krasnoyarsk

Amur

Sapporo

Lake Baikal

KHINGAN RANGE

Vladivostok

Irkutsk

Amur

GREATER

Harbin

Sea of Japan

HONSHŪ

TOKYO

Ulan Bator

SHENYANG

SEOUL

140°

ALTAI

SHANGHAI

MTS.

GOBI (DESERT)

30°

Ūrümqi

BEIJING

Yellow Sea

KYŪSHŪ

Huang

PACIFIC

Zhengzhou

East China Sea

OCEAN

SHAN

SHANGHAI

90°   100°   110°   120°   130°

0   100   200   400   600   800 Miles

0   150   300   600   900   1200 Kilometers

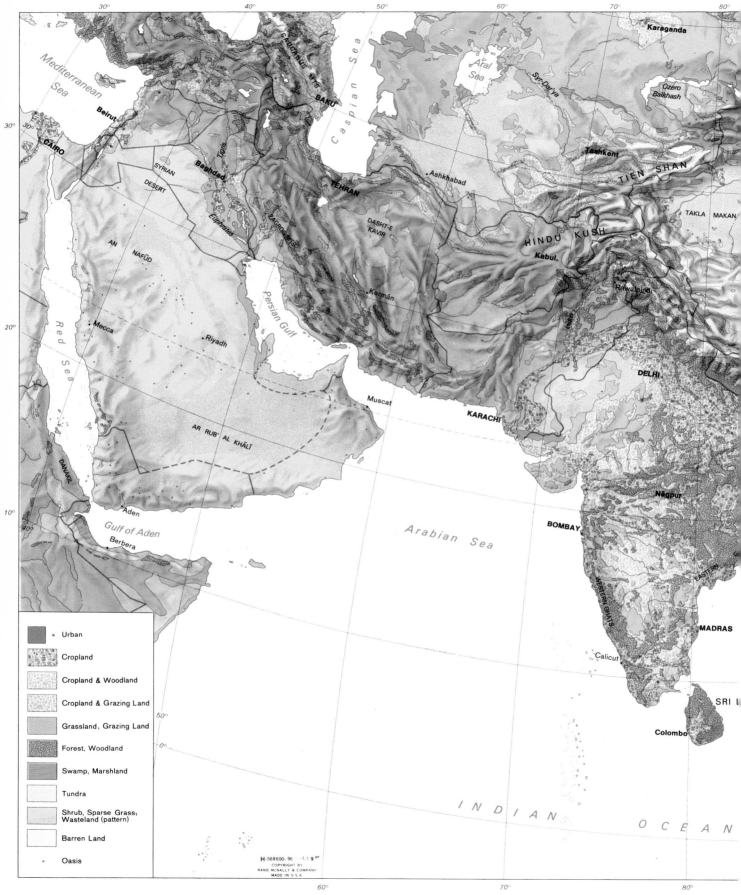

Mediterranean Sea

Beirut

CAIRO

30°

30°

SYRIAN

DESERT

Baghdad

Tigris

Euphrates

AN

NAFŪD

Red Sea

Mecca

20°

Riyadh

Persian Gulf

DANAKIL

AR RUB' AL KHĀLI

Muscat

KARACHI

Aden

10°

Gulf of Aden

Berbera

CAUCASUS MTS

Caspian Sea

BAKU

TEHRAN

ZAGROS MTS

Ashkhabad

DASHT-E KAVIR

Kermân

Aral Sea

Syr-Dar'ya

Karaganda

Ozero Balkhash

Tashkent

TIEN SHAN

TAKLA MAKAN

HINDU KUSH

Kabul

Rawalpindi

Indus

DELHI

Nāgpur

BOMBAY

WESTERN GHATS

EASTERN

MADRAS

Calicut

SRI L

Colombo

Arabian Sea

I N D I A N

O C E A N

■ Urban	•
Cropland	
Cropland & Woodland	
Cropland & Grazing Land	
Grassland, Grazing Land	
Forest, Woodland	
Swamp, Marshland	
Tundra	
Shrub, Sparse Grass, Wasteland (pattern)	
Barren Land	
• Oasis	

H-568600-96 -1-1 9 XP
COPYRIGHT BY
RAND MCNALLY & COMPANY
MADE IN U.S.A.

Scale 1:24,800,000 ; one inch to 390 miles. Lambert Azimuthal Equal-Area Projection

Asia/Animals

Asia, the giant of continents, spreads from far northern lands that are snow-covered nine months a year, to steamy, hot southern jungles. Thus, an enormous number of different kinds of animals are found here.

Most animals of northern Asia are like those in the far north of Europe—reindeer, foxes, hare, and tiny, mouselike lemmings. But in northern China and Korea prowls the thick-furred Siberian tiger, completely at home in cold and snow. The biggest of all cats, it is often as much as thirteen feet (3.96 meters) long.

Cold deserts lie in central Asia, and on them is found the two-humped Bactrian camel. Some of these animals are wild, but many are used as beasts of burden. The Bactrian camel's relative, the one-humped Arabian camel, or dromedary, is found on warmer deserts to the west.

Yaks, huge wild cattle five feet (1.52 meters) high at the shoulder and covered with long, thick fur, live in the high, cold land of Tibet. Many tame yaks are used as beasts of burden by the people of this part of central Asia.

The forests of southern Asia swarm with animals—monkeys, tree-dwelling clouded leopards, small herds of the wild cattle called gaurs, and a dwindling number of tigers. Indian elephants move through the forest in herds of from ten to fifty. Neither as big nor as fierce as African elephants, they are easily tamed, and many have been trained to work for people.

The deadly king cobra, the world's longest poisonous snake, whose bite can kill a human within fifteen minutes, also makes the forest its home. So does the cobra's mortal enemy—the fast, clever, weasellike mongoose which will attack and eat a cobra or any other snake on sight!

In forests on the islands of Borneo and Sumatra lives the red-furred great ape, the orangutan, which may be five feet (1.52 meters) tall. It lives in trees where it swings from branch to branch with its long arms.

And in bamboo forests in a part of Asia where China and Tibet come together lives the famous giant panda. Although it and its relative, the smaller red panda, resemble bears, they are not bears. They belong to a separate family of animals.

Imperial Eagle

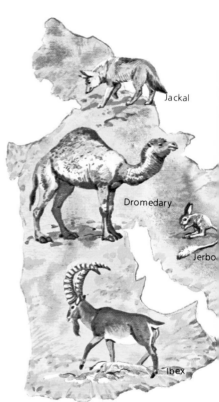

Jackal

Dromedary

Jerbo

Ibex

The largest horns grown by any wild animal are those of a sheep called the Pamir argali, or Marco Polo's argali. Marco Polo found this unusual creature during his travels across central Asia. The sheep's horns spiral outward and have been known to reach a record length of seventy-five inches (190.5 centimeters).

Polar Bear

Killer Whale

Arctic Fox

Willow Grouse

Sea Eagle

Elk

Snowy Owl

Wolf

Harbor Seal

Lynx

Przewalski's Horse

Raccoon-like Dog

Japanese Macaque

Saiga

Yak

Giant Panda

Bactrian Camel

Mandarin Duck

Japanese Crane

Snow Leopard

Pheasant

Water Buffalo

Dolphin

Indian Elephant

Cormorant

Flyingfish

Tiger

Peafowl

Gibbon

Cobra

Macaque

Mongoose

Orangutan

Asia/Countries and Cities

Because Asia is so large, its countries have tended to form in clusters. The continent has five big groupings of nations. The first borders the eastern edge of the continent and is called the Far East. China and Japan are the leading countries in the Far East. Indochina and the islands of Indonesia make up the second group. The third group formed on or near the southern triangle of land which contains India. The desert countries occupy the fourth area. Siberia, a part of the Soviet Union, stands alone in the fifth.

China has the most people of any country in the world—over 945 million. One of every five persons on earth is Chinese!

For endless centuries China was the most powerful nation in the Far East. Then the Industrial Revolution occurred in Europe. Goods and arms were manufactured in great numbers. Suddenly Great Britain, France, and other Western nations had military power. China's growing weakness became clear after the British won the so-called Opium War of 1839–1842. Today, under Communist leadership, China is trying to regain its military and industrial strength.

The industrial giant of Asia is tiny Japan. When Commodore Perry opened Japan to foreign trade in 1853, the Japanese began to adopt Western ways of manufacturing. Today they are third only to the United States and the Soviet Union in industrial muscle.

For centuries Korea was caught between the two big Eastern powers. Both China and Japan had ruled the country. After World War II Korea was once more trapped in battle, with the result that the country is now split. The 16 million people of Communist North Korea look to the Soviet Union as their ally. Anti-Communist South Korea, with 36 million people, looks to the Western nations.

The countries of Indochina, the second Asian group, are also somewhat influenced, culturally, by the Chinese. Indeed, the very word *Viet-*

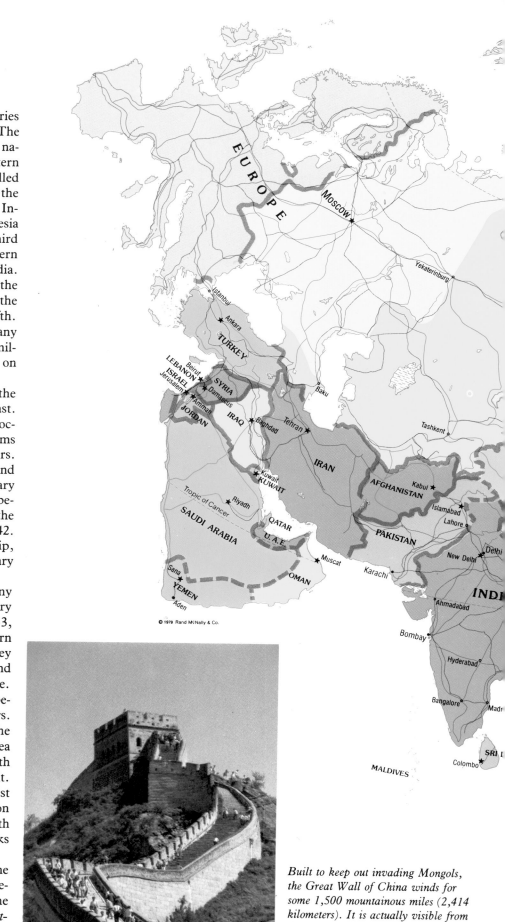

© 1979 Rand McNally & Co.

Built to keep out invading Mongols, the Great Wall of China winds for some 1,500 mountainous miles (2,414 kilometers). It is actually visible from the moon.

nam is Chinese for "far south." Except for the Malay Peninsula at the southern tip, the nations of Indochina formed around river valleys where food grows well. Burma formed around the Irrawaddy River, and Thailand around the Menam. Kampuchea and Vietnam share the lower end of the Mekong River, while Laos grew around a higher part.

Over 153 million people live in Indonesia, making it among the five most populated countries on earth. The Indonesians are scattered over many of the 13,667 islands. They speak a number of languages and have a rather low standard of living. As a result, Indonesia's influence in world affairs is not as great as its population would suggest.

The third grouping of countries is contained on or near the Indian subcontinent. These are India, Pakistan, Bangladesh, and Sri Lanka. All these nations struggle with poverty. India is second only to China as the world's most populated country. Its over 669 million people live in overcrowded cities and villages. In neighboring Bangladesh fewer than ten percent of the people live in cities. The land is fertile, but farming methods are so poor that enough rice cannot be grown to feed the eighty-nine and a half million people of Bangladesh. Hunger visits this part of the world often.

The desert nations occupy the fourth area. People are fewer than in other regions, for there is not enough water for large-scale farming. Turkey has more agricultural land than any other country in the region, but has just 46 million people. Only in Israel, established in 1948 as a Jewish homeland, does the population density reach that of the European countries.

The fifth area of Asia is Siberia, part of the Soviet Union. It has only a few people, who live in widely separated communities. A manufacturing center developed after World War II in the Kuznetsk Basin. A third of the Soviet Union's coal comes from the region —as do farm machinery, chemicals, and building materials.

Civilization is old in Asia. Traditions of the many groups of people who live here had their beginnings in the very dawn of history.

Roads
— Railroads

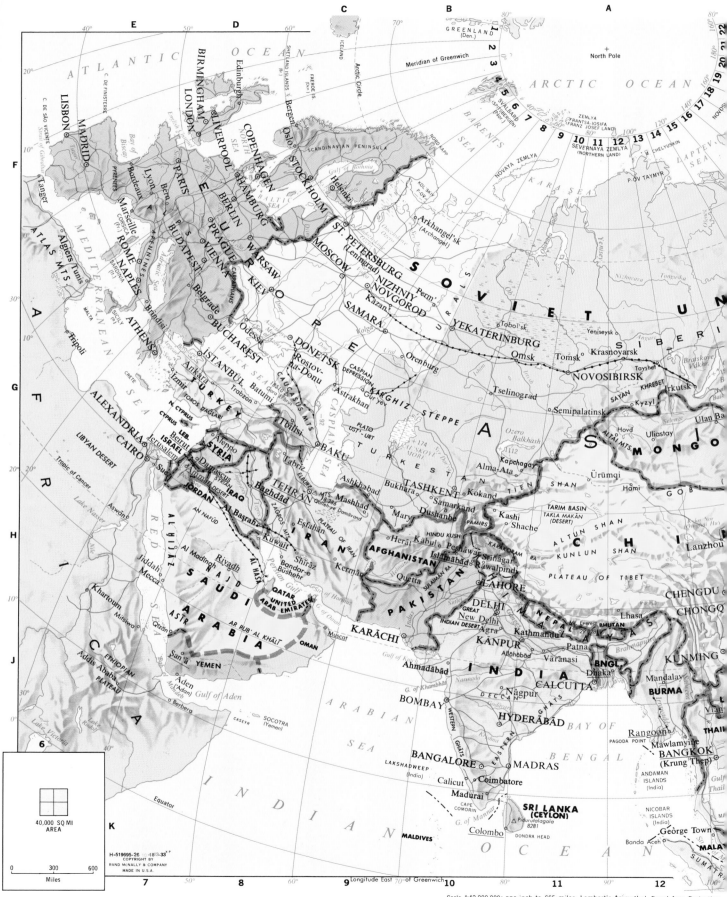

40,000 SQ MI
AREA

0   300   600
Miles

H-519695-26 -18|3-33
COPYRIGHT BY
RAND McNALLY & COMPANY
MADE IN U.S.A.

Scale 1:42,000,000; one inch to 665 miles. Lambert's Azimuthal, Equal Area Projec
Elevations and depressions are given in feet

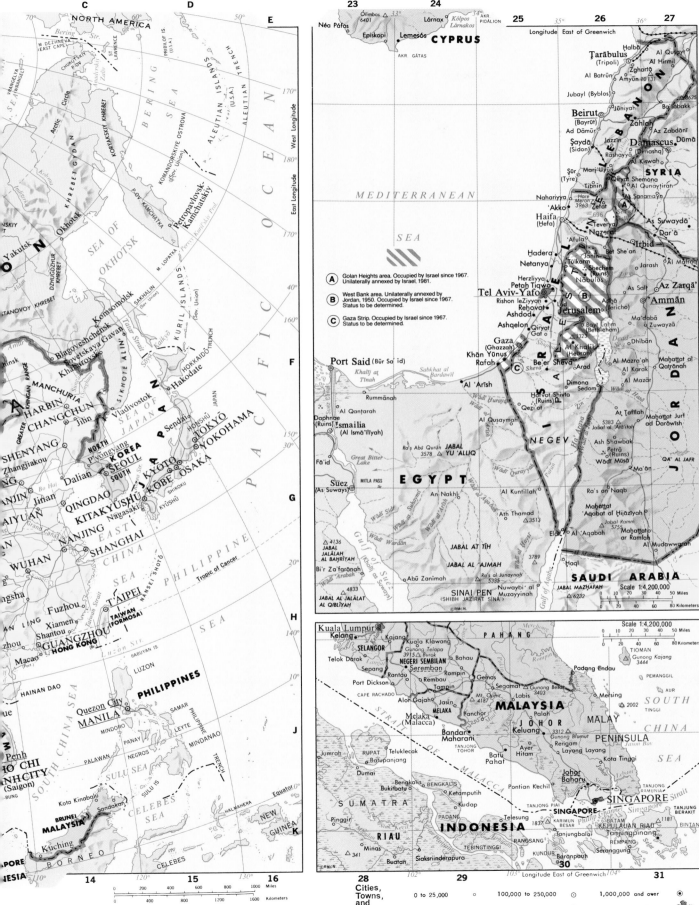

Africa/Terrain

One of the world's great natural wonders is Victoria Falls, on the Zambezi River in southern Africa. They are over a mile (1.6 kilometers) long and with a drop of nearly 400 feet (122 meters)—wider and higher than Niagara Falls.

Africa, the second largest continent, is really a gigantic plateau which stands mostly one thousand feet (304.8 meters) above sea level. It is mostly lower in the north and west and higher in the east and south. On all sides the edges of this great tablelike landmass drop off abruptly to the surrounding oceans and seas. A few narrow coastal plains are to be found—such as those along Ghana, Nigeria, and the Ivory Coast.

Four mighty rivers rise in the high interior. The Niger flows out of wild grasslands where lions roam. The Nile, longest of the world's rivers, drifts past temples built by long-dead Egyptian kings. The Congo drains a dark, humid rain forest. The Zambezi cuts across a vast, thorny woodland.

All of Africa's rivers contain impassable rapids and so are only partly open to boat traffic. For this reason, Africa's mineral and vegetable resources cannot readily be shipped to the cities. This is Africa's great misfortune.

Another problem for Africa's economic development is its smooth and regular coastline. For stretches of hundreds of miles there are no shelters for ships. Swampy coasts thick with stands of mangrove trees make access to the land difficult with their thick jumble of roots standing above the shore. Thus Africa has few good harbors around which a Rio de Janeiro or New York could develop.

Africa has some magnificent mountains. The Atlas Range is a major chain that rims the continent's northern edge for 1,500 miles (2,413.95 kilometers) through Morocco, Al-

Africa's Great Rift Valley cuts a north-south trench 4,000 miles (6,437.2 kilometers) long. In places the valley is broken by plateaus and mountains, but it can be traced by the many lakes and seas which fill its long pockets. The cutaway at right shows some of those bodies of water.

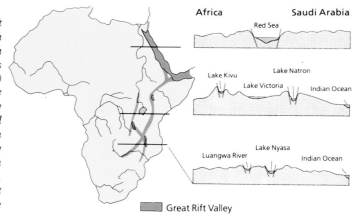

geria, and Tunisia. It was formed at the same time as the European Alps. Both are the result of the collision of Africa with Europe many millions of years ago. After the collision, Africa recoiled, or drifted, back south. The gap between the two continents filled with water to become the Mediterranean Sea.

In East Africa, the peaks of the Ruwenzori Range follow two nearly parallel north-south lines. Among the eastern mountains, snow-crested Mount Kilimanjaro soars to more than nineteen thousand feet (5,791.2 meters)—Africa's highest peak.

Between the high eastern ranges lies the mysterious Great Rift Valley. This is a long rip in the earth's surface where the land dropped down more than a mile (1.6 kilometers). Several beautiful lakes nestle in this rift. Lying on the plateau between the two major branches of the rift is the largest, Lake Victoria, which is almost as big as Scotland.

The Drakensberg Mountains of South Africa are the most unusual range on the continent. As seen from a distance they appear to rise skyward from the earth. Actually, they are not true mountains, just tilted-up portions of the gigantic plateau which makes up Africa.

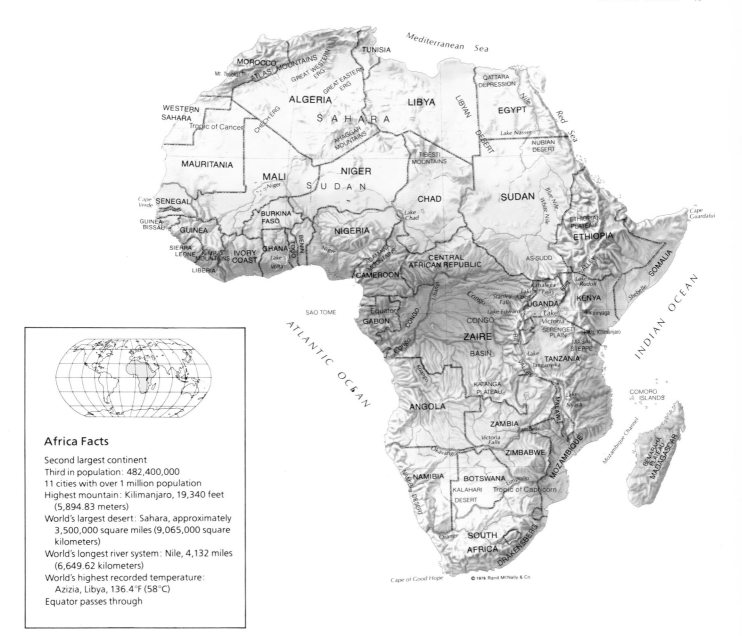

Africa Facts

Second largest continent
Third in population: 482,400,000
11 cities with over 1 million population
Highest mountain: Kilimanjaro, 19,340 feet
(5,894.83 meters)
World's largest desert: Sahara, approximately
3,500,000 square miles (9,065,000 square
kilometers)
World's longest river system: Nile, 4,132 miles
(6,649.62 kilometers)
World's highest recorded temperature:
Azizia, Libya, 136.4°F (58°C)
Equator passes through

Great, windswept deserts cover most of Egypt, a northeast African nation that includes the Sinai Peninsula. Yet, people have learned to live in these dry places.

Few people outside Africa realize just how huge the continent is. More than a hundred Great Britains could be deposited within Africa's borders and there would still be more than enough room for five Frances and four West Germanys. The entire United States could be placed in just the Sahara Desert, which extends for 3,200 sandy miles (5,149.76 kilometers) across northern Africa.

Yet despite its great size, Africa is largely undeveloped. To tap the resources locked within the continent remains a great challenge for its people and for the more prosperous nations which wish to invest in Africa's future.

Scale 1:24,800,000 ; one inch to 390 miles. Lambert Azimuthal Equal-Area Projection

Urban

Cropland

Cropland & Woodland

Cropland & Grazing Land

Grassland, Grazing Land

Forest, Woodland

Swamp, Marshland

Shrub, Sparse Grass, Wasteland (pattern)

Barren Land

Oasis

INDIAN OCEAN

Equator

SEYCHELLES

COMORO ISLANDS

Moçambique Channel

MADAGASCAR

Antananarivo

Tropic of Capricorn

INDIAN OCEAN

Gulf of Aden

Aden

Berbera

DANAKIL

Asmera

Blue Nile

Addis Ababa

White Nile

Mountain Nile

Muqdisho

Nairobi

Lake Victoria

Dar es Salaam

Kisangani

Uele

Lake Tanganyika

Lake Nyasa

Blantyre

Congo (Zaire)

Ubangi

Congo (Zaire)

Kasai

Lubumbashi

Harare

Kinshasa

Lusaka

Luanda

Zambezi

Limpopo

Johannesburg

Durban

KALAHARI DESERT

Orange

Windhoek

NAMIB DESERT

Orange

Cape Town

H-580000-96 -2-2-7×
COPYRIGHT BY
RAND McNALLY & COMPANY
MADE IN U.S.A.

0   100   200   400   600   800 Miles

0   150   300   600   900   1200 Kilometers

Africa/Animals

Africa is a continent of great forests, great grassy plains, and great deserts. Each of these different landscapes has its own special animals.

In the north the enormous Sahara Desert spreads across thousands of miles. Not many animals live in that hot wasteland, and those that do are able to survive with little or no water. In places where scrubby plants grow there are a few small herds of addax, a kind of little antelope with tall, twisted horns. An addax never drinks. It gets the moisture it needs from the plants it eats. The jerboa, a mouselike creature with long hind legs and a long, tufted tail, sleeps in a hole in the sand by day and comes out in the cool night to feed on plants and insects. Jerboas and other little animals and birds are hunted by the fennec, a desert fox.

Of course, the best-known animal of the Sahara is the one-humped Arabian camel, also known as the dromedary. But these animals have actually lived in the Sahara for only about two thousand years. They were brought here from the Middle East. All the camels in the Sahara are used as tame beasts of burden.

Across the middle of Africa is a great rain forest. This is the home of the chimpanzee which moves about in small bands living mainly on fruit and tender, young plants. The rain forest is also the home of the big, burly gorilla, actually a shy and gentle creature. Here, too, are found buffalo, leopards, many kinds of monkeys, and the little okapi, a brown-bodied animal with white-striped legs. It resembles a horse, but is related to the giraffe. In swamps and rivers that lie in the forest area crocodiles swim in search of prey, and bulky hippopotamuses munch on water plants.

Vast, grassy plains lie between the Sahara and the rain forest, and south of the forest as well. Herds of zebra, eland, and gnu, or wildebeest, graze on these plains. Giraffes browse among clusters of trees. Rhinoceroses trot to water holes to wallow in the mud after feeding. Herds of African elephants, the largest of all land animals, plod on their way. Here, too, the spotted cheetah, swiftest of all animals, runs down its prey. And here is heard the shattering roar of the powerful African lion, king of all the beasts.

Tarpon

Addax

Fennec

Pangolin

Colobus Monkey

Despite their fearful appearance, gorillas are generally gentle beasts who eat only plants. They will harm people only if bothered or attacked.

Jackal

Dromedary

Crowned Crane

Eared Vulture

Dorcas Gazelle

Barbary Sheep

Striped Hyena

Crocodile

Greater Kudu

Aardvark

Giraffe

Elephant

Baboon

Chimpanzee

Gorilla

Leopard

Black Rhinoceros

Hornbill

White Pelican

Cape Buffalo

Hippopotamus

Zebra

Lion

Tenrec

Eland

Chameleon

Python

Wildebeest

Ring-tailed Lemur

Cheetah

Impala

Angelfish

Ostrich

Sacred Ibis

Africa/Countries and Cities

Africa today has fifty-three countries. Generally, the countries are grouped in five large areas: North Africa, West Africa, central Africa, South Africa, and East Africa. The countries in each area have some things in common.

Civilization has a long history in North Africa. Egypt was the site of one of our very first cultures. Later the ancient city of Carthage, in present-day Tunisia, was the center of a powerful state that for a time rivaled even mighty Rome.

During the seventh century A.D. the religion of Islam—the followers of which are called Muslims—was adopted by most North African nations. Beautiful Muslim mosques were built in what is now Libya, Algeria, Tunisia, and Morocco. Islam is still the religion of North Africa's people.

Contact between the North Africans and the Africans to the south was made difficult by the sandy and rocky wastes of the Sahara. This desert extends south from the Atlas Mountains and the Mediterranean Sea for nearly 1,500 sunbaked miles (2,413.95 kilometers). Caravans did manage to open a few routes across the desert, and there was some trading for goods and slaves.

Country borders mean little to independent nomads like the Masai people, below. They cross the boundary between Kenya and Tanzania often in search of water and grazing land for their cattle.

Roads
Railroads

© 1979 Rand McNally & Co.

Throughout history North Africa has been distinct from the rest of Africa. Most North Africans are white and speak the Semitic language which in several forms is also spoken by the Jewish and Arabian peoples. Almost one-fifth of all the people in Africa live in the countries of North Africa.

West Africa, much of which is a moist, hot lowland area bordering the Atlantic Ocean, was long known as the slave coast. Through the centuries raiders visited these shores, kidnapped the people, carried them away in ships, and sold them as laborers in many parts of the world. Bitter tales of families torn apart, misery, death, and loss of human dignity are still remembered from this terrible period in Africa's history.

Today, more than one-fourth of the people in Africa live in these countries which border the Atlantic. Nigeria, with over 78 million people, is Africa's most populous nation. Ghana, too, is heavily settled along the western coast.

The equator passes through the continent's third area, central Africa. The most important nation here is Zaire, with about 29 million people. The Congo River and the rivers that feed into it are almost completely contained within Zaire, and the country is almost smothered by a rain forest. The climate is steamy, and insects are not only a nuisance but a hazard to good health.

Eastern Africa is like another world, compared to the rest of the continent. Its western border is marked by mountains which soar above the Great Rift Valley. The climate is far drier than in neighboring Zaire.

The people of Tanzania, Kenya, and Uganda live mainly in these uplands, particularly around the deep water of Lake Tanganyika and the huge expanse of Lake Victoria. Farther north, in Ethiopia, most of the population clusters on the Amhara Plateau.

The continent's fifth area, southern Africa, lies mostly outside the hot regions of the equator. The Republic of South Africa boasts some of the most fertile land on the continent and a climate rather like Europe's. For this reason the land appealed to Europeans. The British and the Dutch fought for

Though many Africans still cling to their old ways of life, modern cities have sprung up across the continent. Nairobi, Kenya, is one such teeming center.

Women carry their wares to market as their ancestors did before them. Colorful cotton cloth has been made in the West African country of Nigeria for centuries.

it. Even though the British army won, the Dutch, known as Boers, stayed on in large numbers. It was the Boers who farmed the rich land and founded successful businesses. Out of a population of over 29 million, four and a half million Europeans control the country.

Europeans also settled the area they named Rhodesia. Rhodesia's black peoples, which make up more than 94 percent of the population, recently took control of the government. They renamed the country Zimbabwe. There has been much political strife in this country.

The fifty-three countries which make up Africa are as different from one another as the lofty mountains of the Great Rift are from rain forests found on the equator. The people of Africa have only begun to control their governments in the past thirty or so years. The countries have only begun to grow. We can only guess where that growth will take Africa.

SPAIN

Cádiz

Str. of Gibraltar
Gibraltar (U.K.)
Ceuta (Sp.)
Tanger (Tangier)
Tetouan
Larache
Ouezzane
Melilla (Sp.)
Beni Saf
Ghazaouet
Oujda
Tilimsen
Saïda

Algiers (El Djazaïr)
Delles
Cherchell
Ech Cheliff
Mostghanem
Oran
Mouaskar
Sidi bel Abbes
Ghilizane
Tihert

Bejaïa (Bougie)
Qol
Lemdiyya
El Boulaïda
Stif
Aïn el Beida
M'Sila
El Djelfa

Skikda
Annaba (Bône)
Guelma
Constantine
Batna
Tbessa
Beskra

Tun
El Ka
TUN

Str. of Gibraltar
Salé
Rabat
Meknès
CASABLANCA
Azemmour
El Jadida
Settat
Oued-Zem
Fès
Taza
Kasba-Tadla
Safi (Asfi)
Essaouira
Marrakech
Jebel Toubkal △ 13665
Demnat
Boudenib
Figuig
Béchar
Aïn-Sefra
Laghouat
El Djelfa
Aflou
Ghardaïa
Wargla
El Wad
Touggourt
Chott Melrhir
Chott Djerid
Gafsa
Cekhira
Gàbes

MOROCCO
ATLAS MOUNTAINS

Agadir
Taroudant
Sidi Ifni
Tiznit
ANTI ATLAS
Igli
Béni Abbas
GRAND ERG OCCIDENTAL
Timimoun
El Menia
GRAND ERG ORIENTAL
Hassi Messaoud
Bordj Omar Idriss
In Am

ISLAS CANARIAS (Sp.)
LANZAROTE
LA PALMA
Tenerife
Sta. Cruz de Tenerife
San Sebastián
GOMERA
HIERRO
GRAN CANARIA
Las Palmas de Gran Canaria
CAP DRÂA
C. YUBY
FUERTEVENTURA

ARQUIPÉLAGO
ILHA DE PORTO SANTO
ILHA DA MADEIRA
DA MADEIRA (Port.)
Funchal

AÇORES (AZORES) (Port.)
GRACIOSA
FAIAL TERCEIRA SÃO JORGE
PICO
SÃO MIGUEL
Ponta Delgada
STA. MARIA
@RMCN.
Same scale as main map

ATLANTIC OCEAN

El Aaiún
CABO BOJADOR
The Western Sahara is occupied by Morocco.
WESTERN SAHARA

Dakhla
Tropic of Cancer
Fdérik

ALGERIA
Adrar
In Salah
PLATEAU DU TADEMAÏT
PLATEAU DU TINGHERT
Illizi

Tindouf
ERG IGUIDI
Chenachane
ERG CHECH
TIDIKELT
TASSILI-N-AJJER
Djanet

EL HANK
Ouallene
TANEZROUFT
Tahat △ 9541
AHAGGAR
Tamenghest

EL DJOUF
Taoudenni
Oued Tamenghe
TUAREG
Mt. Gréboun △ 6562
Iferouâne
Monts Tamgak △ 5906

SAHARA
S

Nouadhibou
CAP BLANC
CAP D'ARGUIN
Atar
Chinguetti
OUARANE
ADRAR DES IFOGHAS
Mabrouk
AÏR
Monts Bagzane △ 6300

Nouamrhar
CAP TIMIRIS
Akjoujt
EL MREYYÉ
Araouane
VALLÉE DU TILEMSI
Kidal
Agadez

MAURITANIA
Nouakchott
Boutilimit
Tidjikdja
Néma
Ouâlata

Saint-Louis
Podor
Dagana
Kaédi
Matam
Mbout
Selibaby
Kiffa
Aleg
Boghé

MALI
Tombouctou (Timbuktu)
Bamba
Niafounke
Goundam
Bourem
Gao
Tahoua
Tessaoua
Madaoua
Maradi
Zinder
Nguru

Louga
Linguère
Nioro du Sahel
Nara
Sokolo
Mopti
Dori
Tillabéry
Niamey
Dosso
Sokoto
Gumel
Hadejia
NIGER

SENEGAL
Dakar
Thiès
Diourbel
Rufisque
CAP VERT
Bakel
Goumbou
Bandiagara
Djenné
San
Ouahigouya
Kaya
Say
Birnin Kebbi
Gusau
Katsina
Kano
NIGERIA

Banjul (Bathurst)
GAMBIA
Kaolack
Tambacounda
Kayes
Bafoulabé
Kita
Koulikoro
Ségou
BURKINA FASO
Ouagadougou
Koudougou
Tenkodogo
Fada Ngourma
Malanville
Kandi
Illo
Kainji Reservoir
Zaria
Kaduna

Ziguinchor
GUINEA-BISSAU
Bissau
Bolama
Buba
ARQUIPÉLAGO DOS BIJAGÓS
Boké
Boffa
Kindia
FOUTA DJALLON
Labé
Timbo
Mamou
Siguiri
Kankan
Bamako
Bougouni
Sikasso
Bobo-Dioulasso
Gaoua
Gambaga
Sansanné-Mango
Natitingou
Kontagora
Zungeru
Minna
Bauchi
Gombe

M'du Tamgué △ 5046
GUINEA
Conakry
Makeni
Kabala
Kissidougou
Beyla
Odienné
Korhogo
Bouna
Yendi
Tamale
Parakou
Sokodé
Jebba
Bida
Jos
Baro
Keffi

SIERRA LEONE
Freetown
Moyamba
Pendembu
Kolahun
KONG
Kong
Dabakala
Boundoukou
Bole
TOGO
Ilorin
Oyo
Iseyin
Ogbomosho
Oshogbo
Ilesha
Ibadan
Ife
Lokoja
Idah
Katsina Ala
Enugu
Makurdi
NIGERIA

Bonthe
Bo
Bori Hills
Robertsport
Mont Nimba △ 5760
Séguéla
Bouaké
Bouaflé
GHANA
Kumasi
Abengourou
Abomey
Savalou
Atakpamé
Abeokuta
Benin City
Sapele
Warri
Onitsha
Aba
Owerri
Dschang
CAM

Monrovia
Buchanan
River Cess
LIBERIA
IVORY COAST
Yamoussoukro
Abidjan
Port-Bouet
Tarkwa
Koforidua
Accra
 Ada
Anecho
Porto-Novo
Lagos
Ijebu Ode
Benin City
Forcados
Port Harcourt
Calabar
Mamfe
Kumba

Greenville
CAPE PALMAS
Harper
Tabou
Grand Lahou
Grand Bassam
Assini
C. THREE POINTS
Saltpond
Cape Coast
Sekondi-Takoradi
Bight of Benin
Brass
Bonny
Cameroon Mtn. △ 13451
Douala
Malabo
BIOKO
Kribi

ATLANTIC OCEAN
GULF OF GUINEA
Bight of Biafra

EQUATORIAL GUINEA
SÃO TOMÉ AND PRINCIPE
ILHA DO PRÍNCIPE
Bata
RIO MUNI
Edéa
Eséka
Campo

Libreville
São Tomé
ILHA DE SÃO TOMÉ

CAPE VERDE
SANTO ANTÃO
SÃO VICENTE
SAL
SÃO NICOLAU
BOA VISTA
SÃO TIAGO
MAIO
FOGO
Praia
Same scale as main map
@RMCN.

Longitude West of Greenwich
Longitude East of Greenwich

A-589100-26 15-15-29×
COPYRIGHT BY
RAND McNALLY & COMPANY
MADE IN U.S.A.

Cities, Towns, and Villages

| 0 to 25,000 | ○ 100,000 to 250,000 | ◉ 1,000,000 and over |
| ● 25,000 to 100,000 | ◎ 250,000 to 1,000,000 | Major urbanized area |

Scale 1:16,850,000; one inch to 265 miles. Sinusoidal Projecti
Elevations and depressions are given in feet

8 9 10 11 12 13

SICILIA (SICILY) **ITALY** GREECE TURKEY
PELLERIA MALTA Antalya Adana
Khania Iráklion Iskenderun Halab (Aleppo)
RHODES (RÓDHOS) Antakya
Al-Lādhiqīyah Dayr az Zawr
NORTH CYPRUS Hamāh **SYRIA** Tudmur (Palmyra)
CRETE (KRITI) Nicosia Hims
CYPRUS LEBANON
M E D I T E R R A N E A N   S E A Beirut Damascus (Dimashq)
IRAQ
Tripoli (Tarābulus) Haifa Amman SYRIAN
Al Khums Al Marj Darnah Tel Aviv-Yafo Jerusalem JORDAN D E S E R T (Bādiyat Ash Shām)
Misrātah Tükrah **ISRAEL** Al Jawf
Zliten AL JABAL Tubruq Dead Sea
Zāwiyat al Baydā' AL AKHDAR Sīdī Barrānī ALEXANDRIA Dumyāt Port Said Ghazzah Al 'Aqabah Taymā'
Banghāzī Sallūm (Al Iskandarīyah) Al Mansūrah AN NAFŪD Ha'il
Surt Khalīj Surt BARQAH Marsā Matrūh Damanhūr Az Zaqāzīq Suez (As Suways) Buraydah
An Nawfalīyah (CYRENAICA) Al 'Alamayn Tantā Jabal Katrina SINAI PEN. Al Jawf
Ajdābiyah CAIRO 8668
Al 'Uqaylah Qasr al Burayqah (Al Qāhirah) **SAUDI**
Sīwah (Oasis) Birket Qarun Al Madīnah
Al Jaghbūb MUNKHAFAD Al Fayyūm Banī Suwayf Būr Safājah **ARABIA**
L I B Y A AL QATTARAH -436 Al-Wajh NAJD
Marādah **E G Y P T** Al Minyā Al Qusayr
Awjilah Wāhat Jālū Al Bawīṭī **L I B Y A N** Asyūt Akhmīm Yanbu'
Zillah Qasr al Farāfirah Sawhāj Qinā Thebes (Ruins) Al Uqsur (Luxor) Al Madinah (Medina)
D E S E R T Idfū
(AS SAHRĀ' AL LĪBĪYAH) Buzaymah S A H A R A Aswān High Dam Aswān RA'S BANĀS
Rebiana (Oasis) Al Jawf Lake Nasser Jiddah Mecca (Makkah)
Ma'tan Bishārah Al Khurmah
Bi'r Misāhah Ash Shabb ADMINISTRATIVE BDY. Halā'ib
Pic Touside 10 712 **NUBIAN DESERT** Jabal Erba 7 274
TIBESTI Emi Koussi 11 204 'Arbī Kosha
Ounianga Kébir 3rd Cataract Dalqū Abu Hamad Būr Sūdān
BORKOU Dunqulah Al Khandaq Kuraymah Marawi 5th Cataract Sawākin Al Qunfudhah Abhā
Largeau Fada Al 'Atrūn Ad Dabbah Kūrtī Barbar Tawkar Taqatu' Hayyā Qizān
ENNEDI 'Atbarah Ad Dāmir Adarama JAZĀ'IR FARASĀN
BODELE Oum Chalouba 6th Cataract Shandī Kassalā Akordat Keren Mitsiwa (Massawa) DAHLAK ARCH. Al Hudaydah
Omdurman (Umm Durmān) Al Khartūm Bahrī Sebderat Asmera KAMARAN
CHAD Mao Khartoum (Al Khartūm) Al Kāmilīn Rufā'ah Barentu Adi Ugri
Lac Tchad **S U D A N** Wad Madanī Al Qadārif Om Hajer
Al Fāshir KURDUFAN Ad Duwaym Sannār Qallābāt Gonder
Abéché DĀRFŪR Al-Ubayyid Kūstī Sennar Dam Adwa Mekele DENAKIL Ed
OUADDAI Jabal Marrah 10 131 An Nuhūd Sinjah Ras Dashen Terara 15 158 Sekota Beylul
N'Djamena (Fort-Lamy) Yao Nyala Al Udayyah AN NUBĀL JIBĀL Roseires Res. Sekota Asmera
Bousso Am Timan Babanūsah Malūt Dangila Debre Tabor **DJIBOUTI**
Talawdī Kurmuk Ambo Farit Dese Djibouti
Sarh CHÂINE Kafia Kingi Bahr al 'Arab Malakāl Kodok Asosa Debre Markos Were Ilu Dire Dawa
Laï Ouanda Djallé DES MONGOS Lol Nāsir AS SUDD Tutu Welel Addis Ababa (Adis Abeba) Harer
Ndélé Yalinga Mashra'ar Raqq **ETHIOPIA** HARERGE
CENTRAL AFRICAN REPUBLIC Rumbek Shambe Nekemte
Fort Crampel BAHR AL GHAZĀL Bor Dembi Dolo Gore Goba Ginir
Fort-Sibut Bambari Tambura Mongalla Gambela Jima S I D A M O
Carnot Fort-de-Possel Rafaï Zémio Jūbā Kapoeta Sodo Wendo Mega Moyale
Bangui Zongo Mobaye Bangassou Gwane Nimule Maji Bako SOMALIA
Mbaïki Libenge Businga Dungu Kitgum Kampala El Wak
CONGO Gemena Bondo Niangara Watsa Arua Mahagi Port **UGANDA** Soroti Eldoret Meru
Dongou Impfondo Lisala Bumba Isiro Gombari Masindi **KENYA**
Ouesso Makanza Basoko Panga Avakubi Irumu Ft. Portal Jinja
Mbandaka **Z A I R E** Isangi Kisangani (Stanleyville) Margherita Peak 16 763 Entebbe Lake Victoria

Scale 1:16,850,000 ; one inch to 265 miles. Sinusoidal Projection
Elevations and depressions are given in feet

The "Homelands" (Bophuthatswana, Ciskei,
Transkei, Venda) were unilaterally created
by South Africa and are not
internationally recognized.

1 Bophuthatswana
2 Ciskei
3 Transkei
4 Venda

7   40°   8   45°   9   50°   10   28°   11   28°30′12

Mt. Kenya
(Kirinyaga)
17,058
Hall
irobi
YA

SOMALIA
Kismaayo
Buur Gaabo
Equator

®RMCN.
Wolhuterskop
Jacksonstuin
Kosmos
Hartbeesport
Swartspruit
Hartbeespoortdam
MAGALIESBERG
Skeerport
Magalies
Hennopsrivier
Foothills
Olievenhoutpoort
Tarlton

Pretoria
North
Pretoria
Silverton
Rayton
Cullinan
4549
Voortrekkerhoogte
Valhalla
Lyttelton
Irene
Tierpoort
Kaalfontein
Halfway
House
Bapsfontein

SOMALIA
Witu
Lamu
Malindi
Takaungu
Mombasa

A

h

26°

INDIAN

Krugersdorp
Randfontein
Roodepoort
5725

JOHANNESBURG
Discovery
Florida
Maraisburg
Alexandra
Edenvale
Primrose
Boksburg
Benoni
5557

Kempton Park
Putfontein

Modderfontein

Brakpan

k

Scale 1:1,050,000
Orlando
Pimville
Turffontein
Rosettenville
Alberton
Germiston
Springs
WITWATERSRAND

B

Port Elizabeth

KAAP RECIFE

Longitude East 28° of Greenwich

®RMCN.

40,000 SQ MI
AREA

0   100   200
Miles

Cities,
Towns,
and
Villages

| | 0 to 25,000 | ○ | 100,000 to 250,000 | ⊙ | 1,000,000 and over | ◉ |
| | 25,000 to 100,000 | • | 250,000 to 1,000,000 | ◎ | Major urbanized area | |

Scale 1:4,200,000

Australia, New Zealand, Oceania/Terrain

The vast expanse of the Pacific is dotted with islands. Some are the tips of volcanoes that push up through the blue waters. Others are atolls, rings of coral surrounding calm lagoons which remain where volcanic peaks have sunk back into the sea. This area includes New Zealand and Australia and is called Oceania.

Australia is the smallest of the continents, yet it has unique features that are world famous—among them the Great Barrier Reef and the "Outback."

The Great Barrier Reef borders the eastern edge of Cape York Peninsula in the north and continues south along the coast for 1,250 miles (2,011.62 kilometers). Coral formations in shades of pink, green, orange, yellow, and purple rise from the ocean floor. Great numbers of different kinds of fish and other sea creatures glide through the tropical waters.

West of the Great Dividing Range, in the central part of the country, is one of the world's lonely desert regions. Australians call it the Outback. Part of it is bush country, where an occasional stunted tree or bush grows.

The mountains of New Zealand's North Island give way in the southwest to hills and then to raised beaches washed by the sea.

Two of Fiji's 800 islands in the South Pacific are large, with lovely tree-lined beaches. Most of the others are merely piles of sand on coral reefs.

Ayers Rock towers 1,100 feet (335.28 meters) above the flat Australian desert.

The rest consists of three main deserts—the Great Sandy, the Gibson, and the Great Victoria. Glaring sun fries the sand, rocks, and clay, and only those animals who have adapted over long centuries to desert life are able to survive.

Rain is kept out of the Outback by the Great Dividing Range. Air moving inland from the Tasman Sea is blocked and forced upward. As it rises it cools and drops its moisture along the coast. The continent's main agricultural area is here. Lush wheat fields and big herds of fluffy-backed sheep have made Australia a leading exporter of grain and wool.

The Great Dividing Range, Australia's main mountain chain, hugs the eastern and southeastern coast for about two thousand miles (3,218.6 kilometers). In the south it dips into the sea and pushes upward again 130 miles (209.20 kilometers) from the mainland to form the island state of Tasmania. The hump-shaped mountains of the Great Dividing Range are old, hammered by the wind and rain for hundreds of millions of years. They are not as spectacular as the Alps or Rockies, yet they have their own haunting beauty, especially in the

deep canyons of the Blue Mountains near Sydney.

The southwestern coast also has low mountains, the Darling Range, which prevent the movement inland of rain clouds. The coastal area is fertile, and wheat and sheep are raised here.

Very different from the arid Outback and the agricultural regions around the eastern and southwestern edges of the continent is Cape York Peninsula in the north. Heat and rain combine here to make ideal conditions for the growth of tropical jungles.

New Zealand is often linked with Australia. But they are individual countries separated by nearly 1,200 miles (1,931.16 kilometers) of lonely ocean, and their landscapes are completely different.

Two main islands make up New Zealand. They are appropriately called North and South Island. Snowy mountains jab upward from almost all of South Island and from much of North Island. On the southwest coast of South Island the mountains send long shoulders into the sea where they form waterways as beautiful as the fjords of Norway.

The most unusual area of New Zealand is the volcanic region around

Lake Taupo on North Island. Here there are boiling springs, geysers with hot water leaping skyward, strange pools of steaming mud, and tiny lakes with beds of brightly colored rocks. Beautiful waterfalls tumble from the encircling volcanic peaks.

South Island, the larger of the two, has magnificent mountain scenery. Glistening glaciers nestle among the heights, and seventeen peaks soar above 10,000 feet (3,048 meters).

The islands of Oceania are thought of in three parts. Most of Polynesia is east of the International Date Line and includes Hawaii, Samoa, Tahiti, and Easter Island. Micronesia in the central Pacific includes the Marshall, Caroline, and Gilbert islands. Melanesia in the southwest includes the Fiji Islands and New Guinea. New Guinea is the second largest island in the world. Only Greenland is bigger.

An expedition headed by Ferdinand Magellan was the first to sail around the world, 1519 to 1522. Crossing the Pacific, Magellan sighted only two islands and finally landed on Guam. There are thousands of islands in Oceania. To have missed all but two was, in a way, a remarkable coincidence!

SINGAPORE

BORNEO

CELEBES

SERAM

Palembang

Banjarmasin

SUMATRA

Java Sea

Ujung Pandang

Arafura   Sea

JAKARTA

Surabaya

JAVA

SUMBA

TIMOR

Timor

Sea

Darwin

Gulf   of
Carpentaria

10°

PEN

INDIAN   OCEAN

KIMBERLEY
PLATEAU

Daly

Victoria

Broome

Fitzroy

Mount Isa

GREAT SANDY DESERT

Alice Springs

20°

GIBSON DESERT

SIMPSON
DESERT

GREA
ARTESI
BASIN

Tropic of Capricorn

Carnarvon

GREAT VICTORIA DESERT

*Lake
Eyre*

FLINDERS RANGES

Kalgoorlie

NULLARBOR PLAIN

*Lake
Gairdner*

Broken
Hill

Murray

DARLING RA.

Great Australian Bight

Adelaide

90°

30°

Perth

	Urban
	Cropland
	Cropland & Woodland
	Cropland & Grazing Land
	Grassland, Grazing Land
	Forest, Woodland
	Swamp, Marshland
	Shrub, Sparse Grass, Wasteland (pattern)
	Barren Land

INDIAN   OCEAN

40°

Scale 1:24,800,000 ; one inch to 390 miles. Lambert Azimuthal Equal-Area Projection

NEW
GUINEA

NEW BRITAIN

Moresby

SOLOMON ISLANDS

Equator

KIRIBATI

P A C I F I C   O C E A N

0°

Coral   Sea

Cairns

Townsville

VANUATU

10°

SAMOA ISLANDS

Pago Pago

NEW
CALEDONIA

ÎLES
LOYAUTÉ

FIJI
ISLANDS

Suva

Rockhampton

Brisbane

Nouméa

TONGA ISLANDS

20°

GREAT DIVIDING RANGE

SYDNEY

Canberra

MELBOURNE

Tasman   Sea

P A C I F I C

OCEAN

30°

Auckland

NORTH ISLAND

TASMANIA

Hobart

SOUTHERN ALPS

Wellington

Christchurch

SOUTH ISLAND

STEWART
ISLAND

Dunedin

A-590200-96 -1-1-7ˣ
COPYRIGHT BY
RAND MCNALLY & COMPANY
MADE IN U.S.A.

40°

0   100   200   400   600   800 Miles

0   150   300   600   900   1200 Kilometers

Australia, New Zealand, Oceania/Animals

Black Marlin

Triggerfish

Butterfly Fish

Cockatoo

Cassowary

Dingo

Death Adder

Tree Kangaroo

Echidna

Emu

Frilled Lizard

Rock Wallaby

Rabbit

Wombat

Great Gray Kangaroo

Koala

Kookaburra

Red Kangaroo

Platypus

Wandering Albatross

White Shark

Slender-billed Shearwater

Black Swan

Many of the animals of Australia are very different from those in other places, for Australia was separated from all other parts of the world for about 50 million years and its animals developed in a different way. Most Australian mammals are *marsupials*. Marsupials are animals like the kangaroo whose babies are kept in a pouch on the mother's body until they are old enough to care for themselves. Two of the strangest Australian animals are the echidna, or spiny anteater, and the duck-billed platypus. They are furry and warm-blooded mammals, but their babies hatch out of eggs!

Much of Australia is covered by a desert or by dry plains, but many animals live in these dry lands. Kangaroos, wallabies, wombats, and bandicoots are among the plains marsupials. One plains dweller, the dingo, is not a marsupial. This wild dog was brought here by prehistoric people. Other desert dwellers include lizards, snakes, and a bird known as the emu.

In the eastern part of Australia lives the koala, a tree-dwelling marsupial. The many rabbits in Australia were brought from England long ago.

On some islands near New Zealand live little reptiles called tuataras. They are the descendants of reptiles that lived before the dinosaurs—the only creatures of their kind anywhere in the world!

Dovey Petrel

Kiwi

Tuatara

Kea

Australia, New Zealand, Oceania/Countries and Cities

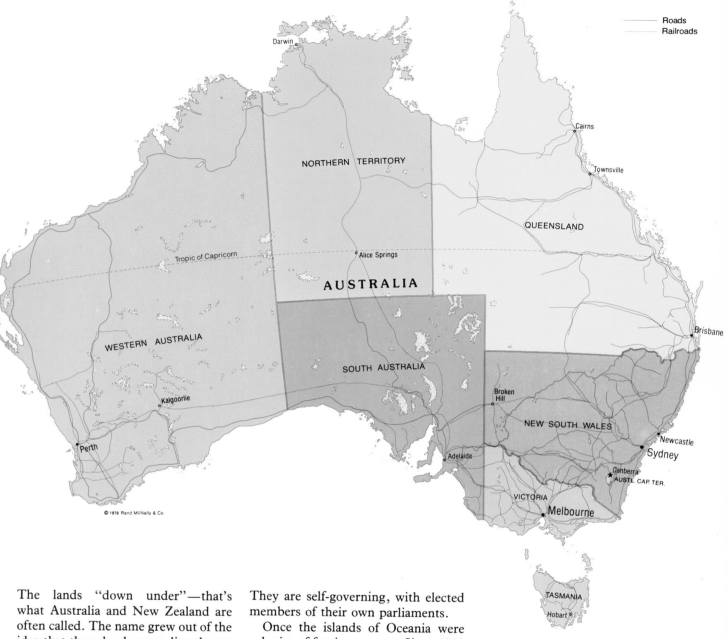

Roads
Railroads

The lands "down under"—that's what Australia and New Zealand are often called. The name grew out of the idea that these lands were directly opposite, under the feet of, Europeans.

In some ways things in the two countries actually are the opposite of those in the Northern Hemisphere. To go north is to head for the warmth of the equator, and to go south is to travel toward cold weather. Winter occurs in July and summer in January. However, only the physical setting is "opposite." Many customs would be familiar to a traveler from Europe or America, for they were handed down by British settlers.

Both countries are members of the British Commonwealth of Nations.

They are self-governing, with elected members of their own parliaments.

Once the islands of Oceania were colonies of foreign powers. Since 1962 many have become independent. The eastern half of New Guinea is a nation. So are Nauru, Fiji, Tonga, Western Samoa, and the Solomon Islands.

In a way, East and West have met in the Pacific. The islanders—descended from Asian ancestors—explored the sea and created highly developed civilizations on some of the islands. Hundreds of years later, explorers from the West "discovered" the lands, and colonies soon followed. Today, remains of the ancient island customs exist side by side with the European way of life.

Pasuruan
G. Mahameru 10,932
12,060
Singaraja
Rinjani
Robbio
Lombok
Sumbawa Besar
SUMBAWA
Waingapu
SUMBA
SAWU
ROTI
FLORES
SAVU SEA
Kupang
ALOR
LOMBLEN PANTAR
TIMOR
Dili
SELARU
TANJUNG VALS

I N D O N E S I A

A R A F U R A   S E A

S U N D A   I S L A N D S

TIMOR SEA

C. VAN DIEMEN
CROKER
MELVILLE
Van Diemen Gulf
COBURG PEN.
WESSEL IS.
CAPE ARNHEM

BATHURST
Clarence Str.
Darwin

S U N D A   T R E N C H

I N D I A N

O C E A N

CAPE LONDONDERRY
Joseph Bonaparte Gulf
Anson Bay
Queens Chan.
ARNHEM LAND
Pine Creek
Katherine
Blue Mud Bay
GROOTE EYLANDT
Limmen Bight
GULF
CARPENT

SIR EDWARD PELLEW GROUP
WELL

BUCCANEER ARCH.
Collier Bay
Sunday Str.
King Sd.
Wyndham
Mt. Hann 2800
KING LEOPOLD RANGES
Victoria River Downs
Birdum
Daly Waters
Barroloola
Newcastle Waters

CAPE LEVEQUE
DAMPIER LAND
Derby
Fitzroy
GEIKIE RANGE
Fitzroy Crossing
Halls Creek

N O R T H E R N
Woods
Alexandria
BARKLY TABLELAND
Burketown

Broome
Roebuck Bay
LaGrange
Stuart Cr.
Tanami
Tennent Creek
Camooweal
Mount Isa
Di

EIGHTY MILE BEACH
LARREY POINT

T E R R I T O R Y
Barrow Creek

Q

MONTE BELLO IS.
BARROW
DAMPIER ARCH.
Port Hedland
RIPON
DeGrey
Roebourne
Marble Bar
Nullagine
GREAT SANDY DESERT
Mackay
Mt. Ziel 4955
MACDONNELL RANGES
Arltunga
Hay

NORTH WEST CAPE
Exmouth Gulf
Fortescue
HAMERSLEY RANGE
Mt. Bruce 4024
Jiggalong
Disappointment
Macdonald
Alice Springs
JAMES RANGE
Amadeus
SIMPSON
DESERT

POINT CLOATES
Onslow
Millstream
Ashburton
W E S T E R N
GIBSON DESERT
Charlotte Waters
Finke
Birdsville

Tropic of Capricorn
CAPE FARQUHAR
Carnarvon
Gascoyne
Peak Hill
Nabberu
Carnegie
Wells
Gillen
MUSGRAVE RANGES
Mt. Woodroffe 4970
EVERARD RANGES
The Alberga
Oodnadatta

BERNIER
DORRE
Shark Bay
DIRK HARTOG
STEEP POINT
Meekatharra
Nannine
Cue
Austin
Sandstone
Yeo
Coopers Cr.
Eyre 39
William Creek
Marree

Ajana
Northampton
Mount Magnet
Laverton
Carey
S O U T H   A U S T R A L I A
STUART RANGE
Farina
Woomera
Pimba
FLI

HOUTMAN ROCKS
Geraldton
Dongara
Mingenew
Moore
Barlee
Menzies
Rawlinna
GREAT VICTORIA DESERT
Hughes
Ooldea Station
Penong
Everard
Gairdner
Whyalla
Port Pirie
Glad
Port Au
Pe

A U S T R A L I A
Miling
Pithara
Lake Brown
Kalgoorlie
Boulder
Coolgardie
Lefroy
Goddards Soak
NULLARBOR PLAIN
Eucla
Point Fowler
Ceduna
EYRE PENINSULA
Moonta
Wallaroo
Part W
Port Lincoln

Mogra
Northam
York
Southern Cross
Cowan
Norseman
Dundas
Eyre
GREAT AUSTRALIAN BIGHT
KANGAROO
Encounter
CAPE JA

Perth
Fremantle
DARLING RANGE
SWANLAND
Salmon Gums
Gulf St.
Kir

DARLING RANGE
Collie
Narrogin
Ravensthorpe
Esperance
Mt

Geographe Bay
CAPE NATURALISTE
Bunbury
Busselton
Katanning
Hopetoun
ARCHIPELAGO OF THE RECHERCHE
I N D I A N

CAPE LEEUWIN
Nornalup
Albany
King George Sd.
PT. D'ENTRECASTEAUX
WEST CAPE HOWE

O C E A N

I N D I A N   O C E A N

40,000 SQ MI AREA

0   100   200
Miles

A-590200-26-   -4-5-13
COPYRIGHT BY
RAND McNALLY & COMPANY
MADE IN U.S.A.

Scale 1:16,850,000 ; one inch to 265 miles. Lambert's Azimuthal, Equal Area Proje
Elevations and depressions are given in feet

Longitude   East of Greenwich
Longitude East of Greenwich

Cities and Towns
0 to 50,000   o   500,000 to 1,000,000
50,000 to 500,000   ⊙   1,000,000 and over

North America/Terrain

In many ways the terrain of most of North America is like that of South America. There is a mass of high mountains in the west, a block of lower highlands in the east, and a huge plain in between.

The western mountains are made up of two main chains that stretch from the arctic shores of Alaska to Panama in Central America. Best known are the Rocky Mountains which rise out of the Great Plains like an enormous blue wall. They are breathtaking in Colorado, where more than fifty peaks soar higher than 14,000 feet (4,267.2 meters).

The Rockies reach northward into Canada, where Mount Robson thrusts upward to 12,972 feet (3,953.86 meters). Here the scenery is wilder than it is in the United States. Evergreen forests cover the mountains' lower slopes. Above timberline—where trees are unable to grow—awesome glaciers crunch their way down stony canyons.

Many separate mountain ranges rise west of the Rockies—the Coast Mountains of Canada, and the Cascades, Sierra Nevada, and Coast ranges of the United States. Inactive volcanoes lie, like sleeping giants, among them. Mount Lassen last moved its mighty shoulders in 1914. Mounts Rainier and ancient Mazama whose hollow core holds the mirrorlike waters of Crater Lake have been dormant far longer. Then in March 1980 Mount St. Helens in Washington, dormant since 1857, erupted with a roar, sending plumes of steam more than a mile high and dropping ash 50 miles away—a reminder that sleeping giants can awaken at any time.

Between the Pacific mountain ranges and the Rockies, in the United States, lies the Great Basin. The Sierra Nevada and the Cascades prevent most of the rain clouds that form over the Pacific from reaching the Great Basin. The dry southern end of this

A great plain spreads across Canada's Prairie Provinces—Alberta, Manitoba, and Saskatchewan. Saskatchewan wheat ripens in the sun.

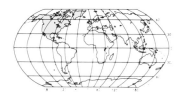

North America Facts

Third largest continent
Fourth in population: 377,400,000
39 cities with over 1 million population
Highest mountain: McKinley, 20,320 feet
  (6,193.53 meters)
World's largest island: Greenland
Location of North Magnetic Pole

A shallow prehistoric sea once covered what was to become Arizona's Grand Canyon. Over millions of years rock layers built up with the rising and falling waters. It took millions more years for the Colorado River to gouge out the canyon.

area is called the Mojave Desert. A desertlike region covers much of the American Southwest and reaches deep into the Mexican state of Sonora.

Mexico also has two main mountain ranges. The Sierra Madre Occidental is in the west and the Sierra Madre Oriental is in the east. Plateau country spreads out between them and it is here that most of Mexico's people live.

Two of North America's well-known volcanoes are in Mexico. They sit side by side in the central region—Popocatepetl, or "Popo" as the Mexicans fondly call it, and Iztaccihuatl. Some people see in Popocatepetl a warrior guarding a beautiful sleeping lady, as the second volcano appears to be. The legends are romantic, but the volcanoes have a fiery past. Iztaccihuatl last erupted in 1868. Popocatepetl has not erupted since 1702, but from time to time it still gives off a puff of smoke—a reminder of the power that lies deep within its boiling core.

Central America, farther south, is mountain country, except for the narrow plains along its coasts. It fairly bristles with volcanoes. There are more than thirty alone in the tiny country of Guatemala.

The uplands on the eastern side of North America are much lower than those in the West, but they have their own charm. In Canada are the Laurentian Mountains. These formed at the edge of a gigantic horseshoe-shaped plateau that surrounded Hudson Bay during the Ice Age.

In the eastern United States the

Mexico's famous Mounts Popocatepetl and Iztaccihuatl can be seen for miles throughout the surrounding countryside. "Popo" is one of America's highest peaks. It is only 2,433 feet (741.57 meters) less than Alaska's Mount McKinley.

largest upland area is the Appalachian chain which reaches from Maine to Alabama. These are old mountains, worn by time and weather. Among them are the White, Green, Blue Ridge, and Great Smoky Mountains.

One of the world's largest plains, the Great Plains, lies in the center of the continent. The land is wonderfully fertile. In eastern Canada farmlands surround Toronto for 150 miles (241.39 kilometers). In western Canada, fields of wheat spread to the horizons. In the United States, the Great Plains form the nation's breadbasket—its wheat-growing lands.

The waters of the Great Plains are

carried away by one of the biggest river systems in the world—the Mississippi-Missouri.

The largest freshwater lake in the world is found on the North American continent. Lake Superior, one of the five Great Lakes, was born during the Ice Age when the glacier scooped out the lake beds.

North America reaches beyond the Arctic Circle in the north. The end of the Boothia Peninsula is the northernmost mainland point. At its southern tip, beyond Panama, it dips to within 700 miles (1,126.51 kilometers) of the equator and joins South America.

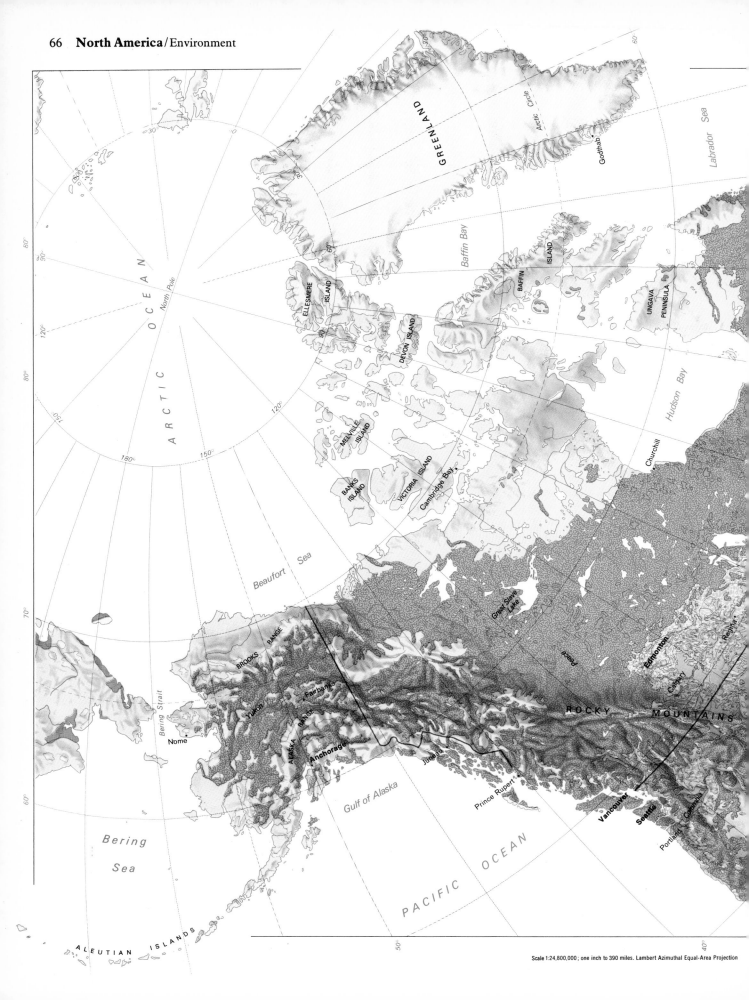

GREENLAND

Arctic Circle

Labrador Sea

Godthab

Baffin Bay

ELLESMERE ISLAND

BAFFIN ISLAND

UNGAVA PENINSULA

A R C T I C   O C E A N

North Pole

DEVON ISLAND

Hudson Bay

MELVILLE ISLAND

Churchill

BANKS ISLAND

VICTORIA ISLAND

Cambridge Bay

Beaufort Sea

Great Slave Lake

Edmonton

Regina

Peace

BROOKS RANGE

Calgary

R O C K Y   M O U N T A I N S

Bering Strait

Fairbanks

Yukon

Nome

ALASKA RANGE

Anchorage

Juneau

Prince Rupert

British Columbia

Vancouver

Seattle

Gulf of Alaska

Portland

B e r i n g   S e a

P A C I F I C   O C E A N

A L E U T I A N   I S L A N D S

Scale 1:24,800,000; one inch to 390 miles. Lambert Azimuthal Equal-Area Projection

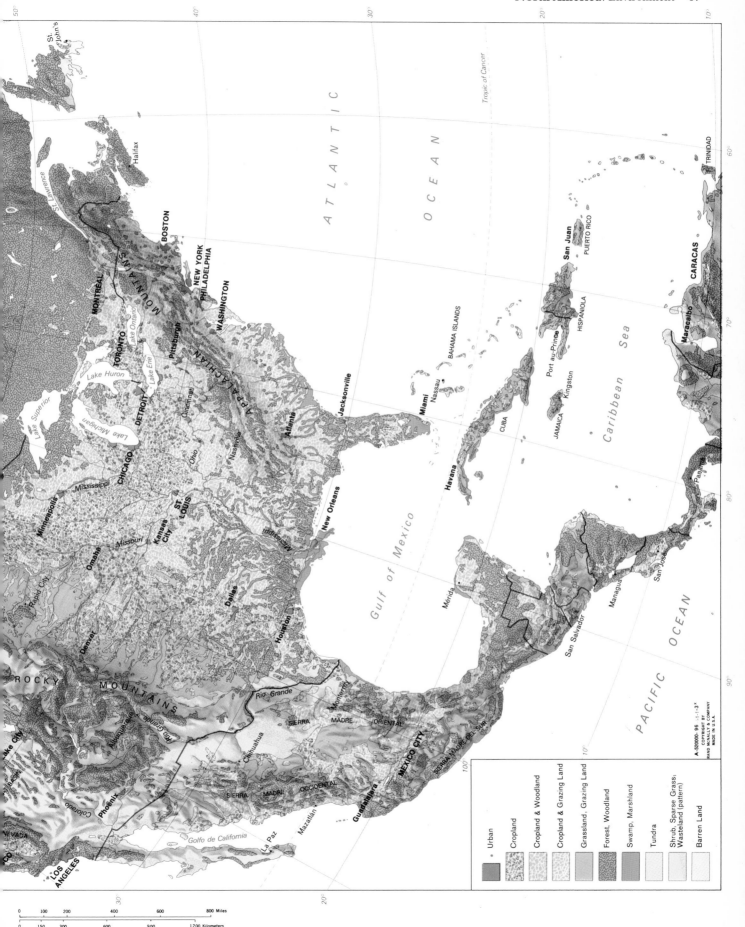

St. John's
Halifax
St. Lawrence
BOSTON
MONTREAL
TORONTO
Lake Ontario
NEW YORK
PHILADELPHIA
WASHINGTON
APPALACHIAN MOUNTAINS
Pittsburgh
DETROIT
Lake Erie
Lake Huron
Lake Michigan
Lake Superior
CHICAGO
Cincinnati
Ohio
Nashville
Atlanta
Jacksonville
Minneapolis
Mississippi
ST. LOUIS
Kansas City
Missouri
Omaha
New Orleans
Rapid City
Denver
Dallas
Houston
Rio Grande
ROCKY MOUNTAINS
Albuquerque
Rio Grande
Chihuahua
SIERRA MADRE ORIENTAL
Monterrey
SIERRA MADRE OCCIDENTAL
MEXICO CITY
SIERRA MADRE DEL SUR
Guadalajara
Mazatlán
La Paz
Golfo de California
Colorado
NEVADA
Phoenix
SALT LAKE CITY
GREAT BASIN
LOS ANGELES

ATLANTIC OCEAN
Tropic of Cancer
BAHAMA ISLANDS
Nassau
Miami
Havana
CUBA
Gulf of Mexico
Mérida
San Juan
PUERTO RICO
HISPANIOLA
Port au-Prince
Kingston
JAMAICA
Caribbean Sea
CARACAS
Maracaibo
TRINIDAD
Panama
San José
San Salvador
Managua
San Jorge
PACIFIC OCEAN

A-500000-96 -1;-1-3*
COPYRIGHT BY
RAND MCNALLY & COMPANY
MADE IN U.S.A.

- Urban
Cropland
Cropland & Woodland
Cropland & Grazing Land
Grassland, Grazing Land
Forest, Woodland
Swamp, Marshland
Tundra
Shrub, Sparse Grass, Wasteland (pattern)
Barren Land

0   100   200   400   600   800 Miles
0 150 300   600   900   1200 Kilometers

North America/Animals

North America once teemed with wildlife. But, in just the last hundred years or so, many kinds of creatures have grown fewer, and some are extinct. However, in national parks, and in deserts and other places where there are few people, many kinds of animals can still be found. And some animals have adapted to living near people and busy communities.

The most "typical" North American animal, the big, shaggy buffalo, or American bison, was once nearly wiped out by hunters. But a few were saved, and today herds of thousands still rumble over the rolling plains in a few national parks.

In the northern woods beavers build dams in streams where black bears catch fish. Porcupines amble through the underbrush, and the lynx stalks its prey. Moose, wapiti, and caribou are found in the north, and far in the north tiny herds of long-haired musk-ox wander.

Packs of wolves still hunt in Canada and the northern United States, but their numbers are growing fewer. However, the smart, bold coyote is growing in numbers, and even prowls the outskirts of towns and cities. Flying squirrels, which only come out at night to glide from tree to tree, and also raccoons and squirrels can be found in almost any wooded area. There are rabbits and chipmunks in every meadow.

Twenty-nine kinds of rattlesnakes live throughout North America. Biggest of them is the eastern diamondback, often seven feet long (2.13 meters). The brightly colored and deadly coral snake lives in deserts in the southwest, together with the poisonous lizard called the Gila monster, and poisonous scorpions with as many as a dozen eyes!

Alligators lurk in swamps and rivers of the southeast. Here, too, live big, hulking alligator snapping turtles that lure fish into their mouths by wiggling a tongue that looks like a fat worm. Another southern animal, found as far south as Central America, is the shelled armadillo which rolls itself up into an armored ball for protection.

A few hundred grizzly bears still roam in the northwest, and that is also where the bald eagle, national bird of the United States, soars in the sky. But both these creatures are in danger of becoming extinct.

Sea otters live in the sea on the west coast. And in a bay on the west coast, thousands of some of the biggest of all animals gather each year to mate—California gray whales, which may be as much as forty feet (12.19 meters) long.

Animals live, thrive, and become extinct. They are known only from their fossil remains. The passenger pigeon, however, was seen and painted by John James Audubon, the great naturalist, in 1840.

Apatosaurus
135 Million Years Ago

Tyrannosaurus
70 Million Years Ago

Woolly Mammoth
10 Thousand Years Ago

Great Auk
Mid Nineteenth Century

Saber-Toothed Cat
1 Million Years Ago

Passenger Pigeon
Late Nineteenth Century

Grizzly Bear

Walrus

Herring Gull

Canada Goose

Polar Bear

Mountain Goat

Red Fox

Gray Wolf

Rock Ptarmigan

Beaver

Porcupine

Bald Eagle

Mountain Lion

Moose

Robin

King Salmon

Pronghorn

Gray Squirrel

Elk

Raccoon

White-tailed Deer

Willet

Sea Otter

Bison

Cottontail

Gambel's Quail

Diamondback Rattlesnake

Opossum

Turkey

California Sea Lions

Peccary

Alligator

Armadillo

Roseate Spoonbill

Brown Pelican

Squirrel Monkey

Gray Whale

North America/Countries and Cities

Canada's houses of Parliament, in Ottawa, stand strangely alone amid winter snow and ice. It is here that 386 members of Parliament meet to govern the country's ten provinces and two territories.

Of all the continents, the boundaries between countries are the simplest in North America. Most of the continent is divided among three nations: Canada, the United States, and Mexico.

Borders between countries are never decided upon easily, and such was the case with those in North America. The boundary between Canada and the United States was settled upon in 1783, following the Revolutionary War, and by treaties in 1818, 1842, and 1846. Today, relations between the two countries are close and friendly. The frontier between them is the longest undefended border in the world, 5,525 miles (8,891.38 kilometers).

The boundary between the United States and Mexico was agreed upon only after the bitter Mexican War of 1846 to 1848, and by treaties and purchases of land.

The United States is the giant among the three countries. It has less land than Canada, but has more than nine times as many people. And it has more than three times the population of Mexico. With its vast stores of raw materials and its industrial know-how, enormous quantities of goods—cars, steel, food, and clothing—pour out of the industrial northeast to the country itself and to the rest of the world.

When the Americans revolted against British rule in 1775, the Canadians remained loyal to the crown. Today, they recognize Queen Elizabeth II as official head of state. Nevertheless, Canada is self-ruling. Although a member of the British Commonwealth of Nations, it has its own parliament and prime minister. Canada, too, is rich in natural resources. It is one of the most prosperous countries in the world.

The way of life of people in Canada and the United States is very much alike. Quite different is the way of life in Mexico.

Mexicans can trace their beginnings back to both the highly developed Indian civilizations, such as the Mayas and the Toltecs, and to the Spanish conquerors. Memories of the Indian peoples who ruled the land before the arrival of the Spanish remain alive in such splendid ruins as Teotihuacán, near Mexico City, which contains remarkable pyramids. Links to Spain are present in the country's many churches and palaces, which are like those of sixteenth century Spain. Customs in Mexico, especially in the cities, are in many ways like those of Spain.

Of all the Spanish-speaking countries, Mexico has the most people—more than Argentina, Chile, and Colombia combined—many more than Spain itself. It carries much weight among the Spanish-speaking nations of the world. Important deposits of oil have been found in Mexico in recent years. With oil scarce and expensive, Mexico's future looks highly promising.

Central America covers an area less than a third the size of Mexico. It is made up of six small republics, the Panama Canal Zone (now part of Panama), and newly independent Belize. Here too, the people's roots are Indian and Spanish. For example, the Indian people of Guatemala are descended from the once-mighty Mayan tribes whose ruined cities still rise in eerie splendor out of the jungles of the north. Indian customs are common in Guatemala. On the other hand, the people of Costa Rica have many Spanish as well as Indian ancestors, and customs can still be traced to the way of life in Spain.

Panama is cut through by the American-built canal, a waterway with an impressive series of locks and dams. It joins the Atlantic and Pacific Oceans, separated only by the twenty-seven miles (43.45 kilometers) of the slim isthmus.

GREENLAND
(DENMARK)

AK
Anchorage
YUKON
Arctic Circle
N.W. TER.
Juneau
CANADA
NEWF.
NEWF.
St. John's
B.C.
ALTA.
SASK.
MAN.
QUE.
Edmonton
ONT.
Vancouver
Seattle
Winnipeg
Montreal
N.B.
N.S.
WA
MT
ND
MN
ME
Ottawa
VT
NH
OR
ID
SD
Minneapolis
WI
MI
Toronto
NY
MA
Boston
CT RI
WY
Detroit
PA
New York
San Francisco
NV
Salt Lake
City
NE
IA
Chicago
IL
IN
OH
Cleveland
Philadelphia
NJ
MD
DE
Washington
UT
Denver
KS
MO
WV
VA
CA
CO
UNITED STATES
KY
Los Angeles
AZ
NM
OK
AR
TN
NC
SC
Dallas
Atlanta
GA
MS
AL
TX
LA
New Orleans
Houston
FL
Miami
BAHAMAS
Havana
DOM. REP.
San Juan
Tropic of Cancer
CUBA
HAITI
Santo
Domingo
JAMAICA
Port-au-
Prince
BARBADOS
MEXICO
Kingston
Guadalajara
Mexico City
BELIZE
HONDURAS
GUATEMALA
NICARAGUA
EL SALVADOR
COSTA RICA
© 1979 Rand McNally & Co.
PANAMA

Mexicans shoot off showers of fireworks and hold gay fiestas to celebrate Independence Day, September 16. Mexico declared its independence from Spain in 1810.

Greenland, the largest island in the world, is considered part of North America. So are the islands of the Caribbean, sometimes called the West Indies. These sunny islands have a colorful past, and stories still are told of Spanish galleons loaded with silver and gold, and of French and British pirates.

English is the main language of North America, spoken by most Americans and Canadians. About a quarter of Canada's people speak French. Spanish and Indian tongues are spoken in Mexico. Spanish, English, French, Dutch, and several other languages are spoken in the West Indies.

European explorers who visited North America once called it the New World. It was indeed "new" to them. In some ways it still is new—or at least young. Cities which thrived before the arrival of Columbus have disappeared. Today North American cities are all more or less like those of Europe. All have come into being only since the year 1500.

B 65° | A BARING Prince Albert Sound | WOLLASTON PEN. | DISTRICT | VICTORIA | BOOTHIA PENINSULA

Old Crow | Eskimo Lakes | Tuktoyuktuk | Amundsen Gulf | MELVILLE HILLS | Dolphin and Union Str. | ISLAND | KING WILLIAM I. | Pelly L.

Porcupine | Aklavik | Inuvik | Ft. McPherson | Anderson | Coppermine | Cambridge Bay | Victoria Strait | KENT PEN. | Queen Maud Gulf | Chantrey Inlet

RICHARDSON MTS. | 140° | 135° | 70° | CAPE BATHURST | 130° | 125° | 120° | 115° | 110° | 105° | 100° | 95°

YUKON | Ft. Good Hope | Coronation Gulf | Bathurst Inlet

Stewart | Mayo | Norman Wells | Arctic Circle | Port Radium | PEACOCK HILLS | Garry | Baker L.

Dawson | FRANKLIN MTS. | Great Bear Lake | Contwoyto | Pelly | Baker

KLONDIKE REGION | OGILVIE MTS. | PELLY MTS. | MACKENZIE MTS. | DISTRICT OF | MACKAY | Clinton-Colden | Dubawnt | Chester

U.S.A. CANADA | Whitehorse | Carcross | Ft. Liard | NAHANNI NAT'L PARK | HORN PLATEAU | Ft. Simpson | Yellowknife | Aylmer | TERRITO | Yathkyed | Rankin

ALASKA | White Pass | Skagway | Watson Lake | Trout | Ft. Providence | Great Slave Lake | Nonacho | Dubawnt | DISTRIC

Juneau | Haines | STIKINE RANGES | ROCKY | CAMERON HILLS | Hay River | Ft. Resolution | Nueltin | THÉ Anne

Chichagof | Sitka | BARANOF | Telegraph Creek | Ft. Nelson | ALASKA HIGHWAY | WOOD BUFFALO NAT'L PARK | Ft. Smith | Uranium City | Selwyn

PRINCE OF WALES I. | Ketchikan | DALL | Fort Nelson | CARIBOU MTS. | Ft. Fitzgerald | Athabasca | Seal | Church

Dixon Entrance | Prince Rupert | Hazelton | Ft. Vermilion | Ft. Chipewyan | Claire | Wollaston | Reindeer | Southern Indian | Granville

MASSET | GRAHAM I. | Smithers | BRITISH | CLEAR HILLS | BUFFALO HEAD HILLS | BIRCH MTS. | Fort McMurray | Cree | Lynn Lake | Thompson | Sipiwesk

Queen Charlotte Islands | MORESBY I. | Burns Lake | Ft. St. James | Peace River | McLennan | CHEECHAM HILLS | Frobisher | Peter Pond Lake | Churchill | MANITO

Ocean Falls | Vanderhoof | Prince George | Grande Prairie | High Prairie | Grouard Mission | Lesser Slave Lake | Smith | Lac la Ronge | Flin Flon | Norway House

CALVERT I. | Quesnel | Wells | SWAN HILLS | Athabasca | Barrhead | ALBERTA | Lac la Biche | SASKATCHEWAN | Cross

CAPE SCOTT | Williams Lake | Whitecourt | Edson | Ft. Saskatchewan | St. Paul | Meadow Lake | PRINCE ALBERT NAT'L PARK | The Pas

Port Alice | Campbell River | Courtenay | 100 MILE HOUSE | Edmonton | ELK ISLAND NAT'L PARK | Wetaskiwin | Vegreville | St. Walburg | Big River | Prince Albert

VANCOUVER ISLAND | NOOTKA | Powell River | Clinton | JASPER NAT'L PARK | Mountain Park | Camrose | Vermilion | Lloydminster | Nipawin | Melfort | Tisdale

Port Alberni | Nanaimo | MT. ROBSON PROV. PARK | Blue River | Ponoka | Wainwright | North Battleford | Saskatoon | Humboldt | Big Quill | Winnipegosis | DUCK MTN. | Swan River | Carmano | Winnipegosis

Vancouver | Duncan | Kamloops | GLACIER NAT'L PARK | MT. REVELSTOKE NAT'L PARK | Lacombe | Red Deer | Innisfail | Wilkie | Biggar | Lanigan | Canora | Wynyard | Yorkton | RIDING MOUNTAIN NAT'L PARK | Dauphin

Victoria | Merritt | Vernon | Kelowna | Revelstoke | Olds | Drumheller | Hanna | Rosetown | Watrous | Kamsack | Melville | Minnedosa | Neepawa | Selkirk

SEATTLE | Str. of Juan de Fuca | CAPE FLATTERY | Penticton | Nelson | KOOTENAY | Banff | Calgary | Bassano | Kindersley | Last Mountain | Qu'Appelle | Russell | Portage la Prairie | Brandon | Winnipeg

Tacoma | Chilliwack | Kimberley | High River | Redcliff | Swift Current | Moose Jaw | Indian Head | Virden | Souris | Morris

Olympia | Grand Forks | Penticton | Cranbrook | Claresholm | Red Deer River | Diefenbaker | Regina | Minnedosa | Boissevain | Morden

WASHINGTON | Spokane | Trail | Fernie | Taber | Lethbridge | Maple Creek | Gravelbourg | Assiniboia | Weyburn | Estevan | Emerson

Vancouver | Portland | Yakima | Moscow | WATERTON GLACIER INT'L PEACE PARK | Magrath | Govenlock | Shaunavon | CANADA U.S.A. | Williston | Minot | Grand Forks

Salem | Pendleton | Walla Walla | Lewiston | Milk | Missouri | NORTH DAKOTA | Fargo

Eugene | Baker | BITTERROOT | Helena | LITTLE BELT MTS. | BIG BELT MTS. | MONTANA | Bismarck | Valley City

OREGON | IDAHO | Salmon | Granite Peak 12,799 | Great Falls | Yellowstone | Billings | Bozeman | WYO. | SOUTH DAKOTA

PACIFIC OCEAN | 125° | 120° | 115° | 110° | Longitude West 105° of Greenwich | 100°

Cities, Towns, and Villages	0 to 25,000 ○	100,000 to 250,000 ◉	1,000,000 and over ◉
	25,000 to 100,000 ●	250,000 to 1,000,000 ◎	Major urbanized area

Scale 1:12,600,000; one inch to 200 miles. Conic Projection
Elevations and depressions are given in feet

Scale 1:12,600,000; one inch to 200 miles. Polyconic Proje

Elevations and depressions are given in feet

O   N   T   A   D   A   Q   U   E   B   E   C

PRINCE
EDWARD
ISLAND

A

NEW
BRUNSWICK

NOVA
SCOTIA

LAKE SUPERIOR

MICHIGAN

B

MINNESOTA

WISCONSIN

MILWAUKEE

IOWA

CHICAGO

ILLINOIS

C

MISSOURI

INDIANA

OHIO

PITTSBURGH

PENN.

NEW YORK

PHILADELPHIA

BALTIMORE

KENTUCKY

WEST
VIRGINIA

VIRGINIA

WASHINGTON
D.C.

MD.

DEL.

N.J.

TENNESSEE

NORTH CAROLINA

D

ARKANSAS

MISSISSIPPI

ALABAMA

GEORGIA

SOUTH
CAROLINA

LOUISIANA

FLORIDA

E

GULF OF MEXICO

ATLANTIC OCEAN

BAHAMAS

MIAMI

Key West

Cities
and
Towns

| 0 to 50,000 | ○ | 500,000 to 1,000,000 | ◉ |
| 50,000 to 500,000 | ⊙ | 1,000,000 and over | |

40,000 SQ MI
AREA

0   100   200

Miles

ATLANTIC OCEAN

Aguadilla Arecibo San Juan CABEZAS DE SAN JUAN ST. THOMAS TORTOLA (Br.)

PTA. HIGUERO Utuado Bayamón Fajardo CULEBRA Charlotte Amalie ST. JOHN (U.S.A.)

Mayagüez PUERTO RICO (U.S.A.) Caguas Humacao VIEQUES

Coamo Cayey

CABO ROJO Ponce Salinas Guayama Christiansted

CARIBBEAN SEA SAINT CROIX (U.S.A.)

Scale 1:4,300,000
0 10 20 30 40 Miles
0 10 20 30 40 50 60 Kilometers
©RMcN

LITTLE HANS LOLLICK
INNER BRASS OUTER BRASS HANS LOLLICK
STORMY PT. PICARA PT. GRASS CAY
THATCH CAY
ST. THOMAS Crown Mt. (U.S.A.) 1558 Charlotte Amalie (St. Thomas) Nadir
WATER FLAMINGO PT. St. Thomas Harbor
©RMcN Scale 1:5,400,000

W.VIRGINIA Richmond
Roanoke Chesapeake Bay
VIRGINIA Norfolk
Mt. Mitchell 6684 NORTH CAROLINA
Raleigh
Charlotte CAPE HATTERAS
SOUTH CAROLINA Wilmington
Columbia CAPE FEAR
Augusta Charleston
GEORGIA Savannah
Jacksonville
St. Augustine BERMUDA (Br.)
Ocala
Tampa Bay CAPE CANAVERAL
FLORIDA
MIAMI W. Palm Beach
CAPE SABLE Lake Okeechobee
Key West GRAND BAHAMA GREAT ABACO
FLORIDA KEYS Straits of Florida Nassau ELEUTHERA CAT
ANDROS SAN SALVADOR (WATLING)
LONG
HAVANA Guanabacoa Matanzas
Cárdenas Santa Clara Sancti Spíritus
del Río Cienfuegos Trinidad Ciego de Avila
ISLA DE LA JUVENTUD CUBA Camagüey Nuevitas
Manzanillo Holguín PUNTA MAISI
GRAND CAYMAN (Br.) SIERRA MAESTRA Guantánamo Cap-Haïtien Puerto Plata C. SAMANA
Santiago de Cuba Santiago de los Caballeros 28 374
C. CRUZ ÎLE DE LA GONAVE HAITI DOMINICAN Sánchez Mayagüez San Juan
Montego Bay Mt. Denham 2236 Port Antonio Pico Duarte 10 417 REPUBLIC Ponce Charlotte Amalie
Spanish Town Port-au-Prince Santo Domingo PUERTO RICO (U.S.A.) ANGUILLA
JAMAICA Kingston HISPANIOLA BARBUDA (Ant.)
ANTILLES SAINT CROIX (U.S.A.) ANTIGUA AND BARBUDA
ST. KITTS AND NEVIS MONTSERRAT (Br.) Pointe-à-Pitre
V. Soufrière 4869 GUADELOUPE (Fr.)
Basse-Terre DOMINICA
MARTINIQUE (Fr.) Fort-de-France
ST. LUCIA
CARIBBEAN SEA ST. VINCENT AND THE GRENADINES BARBADOS
Kingstown Bridgetown
GRENADA
PUNTA DE GALLINAS SAN ROMAN TOBAGO
PENÍNSULA DE GUAJIRA ARUBA (Neth.) CURAÇAO (Neth.) BONAIRE (Neth.) ISLA LA TORTUGA ISLA DE MARGARITA TRINIDAD AND TOBAGO
Santa Marta Golfo de Venezuela Willemstad Coro Carúpano Port of Spain
Barranquilla Ciénaga Maracaibo San Felipe Puerto Cabello La Guaira Cumaná TRINIDAD
Cartagena Soledad Cabimas CARACAS Puerto la Cruz
AMERICA Lago de Maracaibo Barquisimeto Maracay Valencia Maturín
Limón Colón Valera Guanare Calabozo El Tigre
David PANAMA Porfobelo Golfo del Darién Trujillo San Fernando de Apure Ciudad Guayana Morawhanna
Santiago Antón Panamá Lorica Sincelejo Magangué Mérida Puerto de Nutrias Río Ciudad Bolívar
PEN. DE AZUERO Golfo de Panamá Montería Ocaña VENEZUELA Cerro Bolívar
Cúcuta San Cristóbal Cerro Icutu 7800
Barrancabermeja Pamplona
Medellín Bucaramanga GUYANA
Sonsón Tunja Meta
Manizales COLOMBIA
Pereira Armenia SANTA FE DE BOGOTA San Fernando de Atabapo
ISLA DE MALPELO (Colombia) Ibagué Girardot Villavicencio SERRA PACARAIMA
Buenaventura Cali Palmira Guaviare Orinoco BRAZIL

13
40 000 SQ MI AREA
0 100 200
Miles

8 80° 9 75° Longitude West of Greenwich 10 70° 11 60° 12

Almost in the clouds is Lake Titicaca, on a windswept plateau in the Andes. It is South America's largest lake—3,500 square miles (9,065 square kilometers)—and the highest large lake in the world.

Mountains span the length of South America like a gigantic, rocky backbone. Though scarcely 200 miles (321.86 kilometers) wide in some places, the Andes chain is the longest in the world. It stretches over four thousand miles (6,437.2 kilometers) along the continent's west coast. This range also boasts some of the earth's tallest peaks. Only Asia's Himalaya Mountains are higher than Mount Aconcagua, which frowns down on western Argentina.

Over three-fourths of South America lies in the tropics. The Andes, however, have a climate all their own. Low down, where they break out of the eastern flatlands, the air is hot and tropical plants can grow. Above 7,000 feet (2,133.6 meters) the air becomes cooler. Great forests thrive, giving way at slightly higher altitudes to crop and grazing land. Here the Incas and other Indian peoples built their great civilizations. Beyond, to the frozen snowline, the air grows gradually colder. Above 13,000 feet (3,962.4 meters),

only moss, lichens, and tough, grasslike plants, called sedge, survive.

Where Argentina, Bolivia, and Chile meet, the Andes split into two ranges. They are separated by a windswept plateau about 400 miles (643.72 kilometers) wide. This is the Altiplano, as it is called in Spanish, or "high plateau." It is nearly two and a half miles (4.02 kilometers) above sea level and almost perfectly flat—a strange sight nestled between the towering peaks.

Many rivers and streams tumble from the Andes and other highland areas. The great Amazon River begins in the Andes of Peru and flows 3,900 miles (6,276.27 kilometers) to the Atlantic Ocean. The Amazon contains more water than any river on earth—over 4 million cubic feet (113,200 cubic meters) pour into the Atlantic each second! Small ships can sail more than two thousand miles (3,218.6 kilometers) upstream to the foot of the Andes.

Other major rivers include the

Magdalena in Colombia, the São Francisco in east Brazil, and the Orinoco, life stream of Venezuela. Another, the Paraguay-Paraná, flows southward through Brazil, Paraguay, and Argentina. In South America, only the Amazon is longer and contains more water.

The Amazon carries water away from a huge plain called the Amazon Basin—an area almost as big as forty-eight of the fifty United States! This basin is one of two major flatlands in South America. Its heat and rainy downpours support hundreds of miles of densely packed trees, making the Amazon the world's largest rain forest.

Quite different from the first plain is the second. It stretches across Paraguay and most of Argentina, and is made up of two distinct areas—the Gran Chaco and the Pampa. The Gran Chaco is a dry region with scrubby trees widely spaced. Farther south and closer to the coast, rainfall supports the Pampa, a nearly treeless grassland ideal for cattle and sheep grazing.

The grassy Pampa gives way in the south to a strip of dry, shrubby land known as Patagonia, which covers most of South America's narrow tail. Only the Atacama Desert, between the Chilean Andes and the Pacific Ocean, is more barren.

Aside from the Andes, South America contains two other upland areas. The Brazilian Highlands separate the Amazon Basin from the Gran Chaco and reach nearly two thousand miles (3,218.6 kilometers) inland from the Atlantic. In places they are quite rugged, with spectacular waterfalls that drop over scenic cliffs. Iguassu Falls is one of the most breathtaking. Waters from its 275 falls crash thunderously over a rocky expanse more than one and a half miles (2.41 kilometers) wide.

Despite the many rivers which empty themselves along South America's 5,000-mile (24,140-kilometer) coastline, the continent has few good natural harbors. Even fewer islands hug its shores. The only large ones are Trinidad and Tobago, off Venezuela, and the Galápagos, west of Ecuador. A string of smaller islands follows the coast of Chile south to Tierra del Fuego. Here the continent ends as the Andes sink their slopes into the sea.

South America Facts

Fourth largest continent
Fifth in population: 243,100,000
18 cities with over 1 million population
Highest mountain: Aconcagua, 22,831 feet
  (6,958.88 meters)
World's highest waterfall: Angel Falls, 3,700
  feet (1,127.76 meters)
Equator passes through

All of the world's natural sodium nitrate is blasted from the Atacama Desert, which stretches 600 miles (965.58 kilometers) along the coast of Chile. Nitrate is used to make fertilizer and explosives.

South America's Amazon River contains more water than the Nile, Yangtze, and Mississippi rivers combined—or nearly one-fifth of all the fresh water that runs off the earth's surface. Its outpouring is so great that the water of the open sea is fresh for over 200 miles (321.86 kilometers) beyond the river's mouth.

Tropic of Cancer

ATLANTIC   OCEAN

Havana

CUBA

BAHAMAS

HISPANIOLA

Kingston

JAMAICA

San Juan

PUERTO
RICO

Caribbean Sea

Panamá

Barranquilla

Maracaibo

CARACAS

Port of Spain

TRINIDAD

Georgetown

SANTA FE DE BOGOTA

Quito

Iquitos

LIMA

La Paz

ANDES

Orinoco

Negro

Manaus

Amazon

SELVAS

Rio Branco

Belém

Equator

Fortaleza

Recife

São Francisco

Salvador

Brasília

Cuiabá

MATO
GROSSO

Scale 1:24,800,000; one inch to 390 miles. Lambert Azimuthal Equal-Area Projection

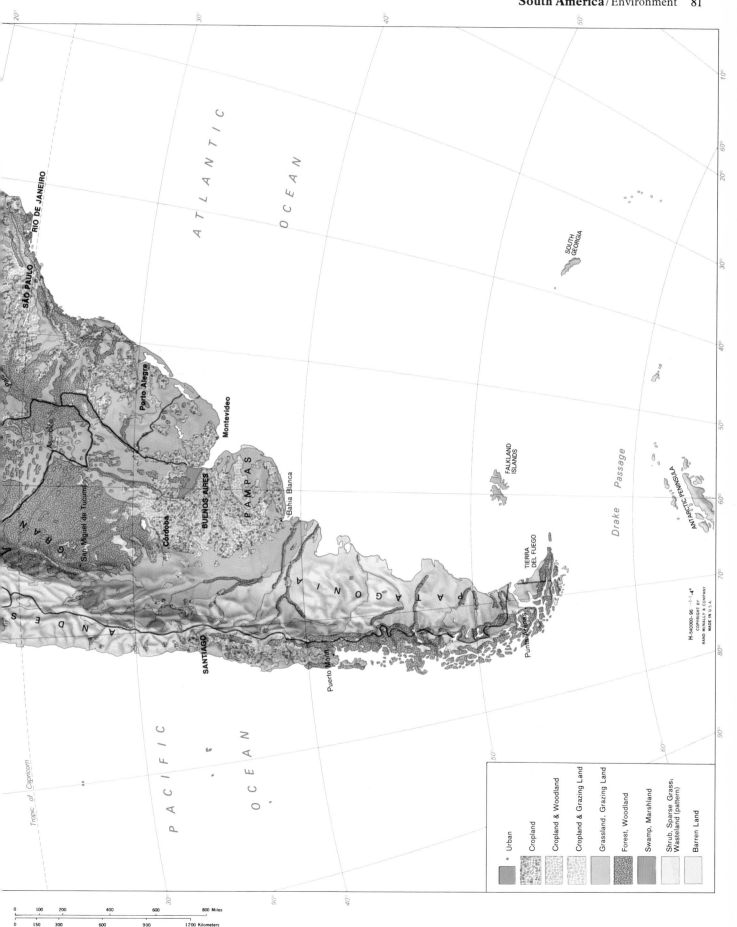

20°

30°

40°

50°

10°

60°

20°

30°

40°

50°

A T L A N T I C

O C E A N

RIO DE JANEIRO

SÃO PAULO

Porto Alegre

Montevideo

Asunción

BUENOS AIRES

Córdoba

San Miguel de Tucumán

G R A N

PAMPAS

Bahia Blanca

P A T A G O N I A

A N D E S

SANTIAGO

Puerto Mont

Punta Arenas

TIERRA
DEL FUEGO

SOUTH
GEORGIA

FALKLAND
ISLANDS

Drake Passage

ANTARCTIC PENINSULA

60°

70°

80°

Tropic of Capricorn

P A C I F I C

O C E A N

50°

90°

40°

90°

60°

H-540000-96 ·-1·-1·4·*
COPYRIGHT BY
RAND MCNALLY & COMPANY
MADE IN U.S.A.

•	Urban
	Cropland
	Cropland & Woodland
	Cropland & Grazing Land
	Grassland, Grazing Land
	Forest, Woodland
	Swamp, Marshland
	Shrub, Sparse Grass; Wasteland (pattern)
	Barren Land

0   100   200   400   600   800 Miles

0   150   300   600   900   1200 Kilometers

South America/Animals

Vast tropical forests spread over much of South America and are the home of a great number of creatures. The big, spotted cats called jaguars prowl among the trees by night, and herds of little piglike peccaries root in the underbrush. One kind of large, hoglike tapir lives here. It is related to both the horse and rhinoceros, and its nose ends in a short trunk.

Many creatures live up in the trees. Little, long-legged sloths, hanging upside down from branches, inch along as they feed on leaves. Monkeys shriek, howl, whistle, and chatter from the treetops—red uakaris, that look like sad old men; long-tailed, black-furred woolly monkeys; large-eyed douroucoulis; and golden marmosets. Brightly colored parrots, macaws, toucans, and other birds flash from tree to tree.

In the rivers swim caimans, the alligators of South America, and many fish including the vicious, flesh-eating piranha, with its razor-sharp teeth. A school of piranhas can devour an animal down to the bare bones in a matter of minutes! Anacondas, giant snakes often more than thirty feet (9.14 meters) long, lurk in some rivers, waiting to seize unwary animals that come to the shores to drink.

On the plains of South America live bushy-furred giant anteaters, which may be more than six feet (1.82 meters) long from tip of nose to end of tail. Here, too, are found long-legged maned wolves, which have been described as looking like a fox walking on stilts.

Many animals live in the long range of mountains along the west coast. This is where the humpless camels of South America are mostly found—llamas, alpacas, guanacos, and vicuñas—small, heavily furred beasts that live in herds. The spectacled bear roams the mountain slopes. It gets its name from the circles of yellowish fur, like eyeglass frames, around its eyes. The chinchilla, a bushy-tailed, mouselike creature with the finest, silkiest fur in the world, lives high up on the snow-capped heights. And gliding through the air between mountain peaks is the great South American condor with a wingspread of nearly ten feet (3.04 meters). It is a kind of vulture that feeds on dead animals.

Nearly a fourth of all the world's animals live in South America. Because forests are rapidly being cleared, and plains used for farming and grazing, many of these animals are in serious danger of becoming extinct.

The mysterious Galápagos Islands lie about 600 miles (965.58 kilometers) off the coast of Ecuador. Here live rare cormorants that cannot fly, great lizardlike iguanas, and giant turtles weighing over 500 pounds (226.8 kilograms).

Sloth

Tapir

Manatee

Scarlet Ibis

Coatimundi

Ocelot

Piranha

Green
Turtle

Toucan

Caiman

Spectacled
Bear

Anaconda

Vampire Bat

Llama

Spider Monkey

Red Brocket
Deer

Howling
Monkey

Macaw

Chinchilla

Capybara

Jaguar

Great Anteater

Vicuña

Brazilian
Lapwing

Condor

Guanaco

Maned Wolf

Alpaca

Pampas Deer

Blue Marlin

Torrent
Duck

Rhea

Elephant
Seal

Magellan
Goose

Magellan
Penguin

Cavy

Black-necked
Swan

Sperm Whale

South America/
Countries and Cities

Roads
Railroads

Barranquilla
Caracas
Port of Spain
★ TRINIDAD AND TOBAGO
Maracaibo
VENEZUELA
Georgetown
Paramaribo
GUYANA
Cayenne
SURINAME
FR.
GUIANA
Santa Fe de Bogotá ★
COLOMBIA
Equator
ECUADOR ★ Quito
Manaus
Belem
Guayaquil
Fortaleza
PERU
BRAZIL
Recife
Lima
Cuzco
La Paz
Salvador
BOLIVIA
Brasilia
Sucre
Belo Horizonte
Tropic of Capricorn
PARAGUAY
Antofagasta
Asuncion
Sao Paulo
Rio de Janeiro
Santos
Pôrto Alegre
CHILE
Cordoba
Valparaiso
Mendoza
Rosario
URUGUAY
Santiago
Buenos Aires
Montevideo
La Plata
Concepcion
ARGENTINA
Bahia Blanca
FALKLAND
ISLANDS
(U.K.)
Punta Arenas

South America is but one name for a continent which today is divided into twelve independent nations. Along with its Central American and Mexican neighbors, South America is often called Latin America.

Most South Americans speak either Spanish or Portuguese—tongues based on the language of ancient Rome, or *Latium*. Europeans brought these Latin languages with them when they conquered the continent in the mid-1500s. Spanish is the official language of all but three of the continent's twelve nations. Portuguese is spoken in Brazil, South America's largest and most populated country.

Brazil spreads over half the continent and is one of the world's biggest nations. Only the Soviet Union, China, Canada, and the United States are larger in area. Almost 124 million people live in Brazil, more than in all other South American countries combined.

Brazil is a nation on the go. São Paulo, to the south, is the major industrial city of the continent. Factories are going up in ever-increasing numbers, particularly in the coastal region between São Paulo and Rio de Janeiro.

Two small nations north of Brazil also have official languages other than Spanish. The Dutch-speaking people of Suriname and the English-speaking people of Guyana have ancestors who were mainly Hindustanis—people from India—or black Africans. These groups were brought to South America by the Dutch and English during colonial days to work

High in the Andes near Cuzco, Peru, lie the ruins of Machu Picchu—once a walled Incan city. Unknown to the Spanish, it may have been a last hideaway for the doomed Inca people.

on sugar plantations along the marshy coast.

Ninety percent of the people in neighboring French Guiana are black or of mixed African and European ancestry. French is the official language, for French Guiana really belongs to faraway France. In years past, French Guiana was famous for its prison colony on Devils Island, and for the dreaded prison camps at Kourou and Saint-Laurent on the mainland. These camps were closed in 1945.

Spanish-speaking Argentina, to the far south, differs greatly from these three small pockets of northern settlements. After Brazil, Argentina is the largest South American nation in both area and population. The country sprawls over 1,072,162 square miles (413,961.74 square kilometers) and contains around 27 million people. Its lifeblood is the Pampa, a huge plain where rich soil supports fields of grain and grass feeds great herds of cattle.

Argentina has attracted large numbers of Europeans. Its capital, Buenos Aires, has mushroomed until the population of the city and its suburbs tilts toward ten and a half million.

Argentina is especially powerful among the nations of the southern part of the continent. These include Chile, whose over 11 million people live in the narrow strip of land between the Pacific and the Andes, and Uruguay and Paraguay, tiny countries with fewer than three and a half million citizens apiece.

The more northern countries of Peru, Ecuador, and Bolivia have much in common, for their Andean plateaus and valleys once belonged to the golden empire of the Incas. The Incas ruled over a highly civilized realm of about 3 million subjects. Today, Peru alone has over 8 million Indian citizens—more than any other country in the Western Hemisphere. Many Indians still speak Quechua—the language of the ancient Incas.

Cuzco, in modern-day Peru, was the capital of the empire. Still standing is the fortress which crowned the ancient city. Its walls consist of such massive boulders that scientists cannot understand how the Incas were able to build with them.

Farther north along the Pacific coast is Colombia, gateway to the continent. Only through Colombia can land travelers reach Central America. Bogotá, Colombia's capital and largest city, was among the first settled in the New World.

For years neighboring Venezuela was one of South America's poorest nations. But all this changed when, in 1917, vast oil deposits were discovered at Maracaibo. Today, Venezuela has the highest standard of living in South America. And, Venezuela and Ecuador are Latin America's only members of the powerful Organization of Petroleum Exporting Countries (OPEC).

But whatever their power, location, or size, the countries of South America are linked by the strong Latin character of their continent. This tie sets them apart from the people of any other single continent.

Chile possesses a wealth of minerals. It mines about 16 percent of the world's copper and vast amounts of iron ore, nitrates, and coal.

Brazil's capital is the ultra-modern city of Brasília, built in 1960 in the central uplands.

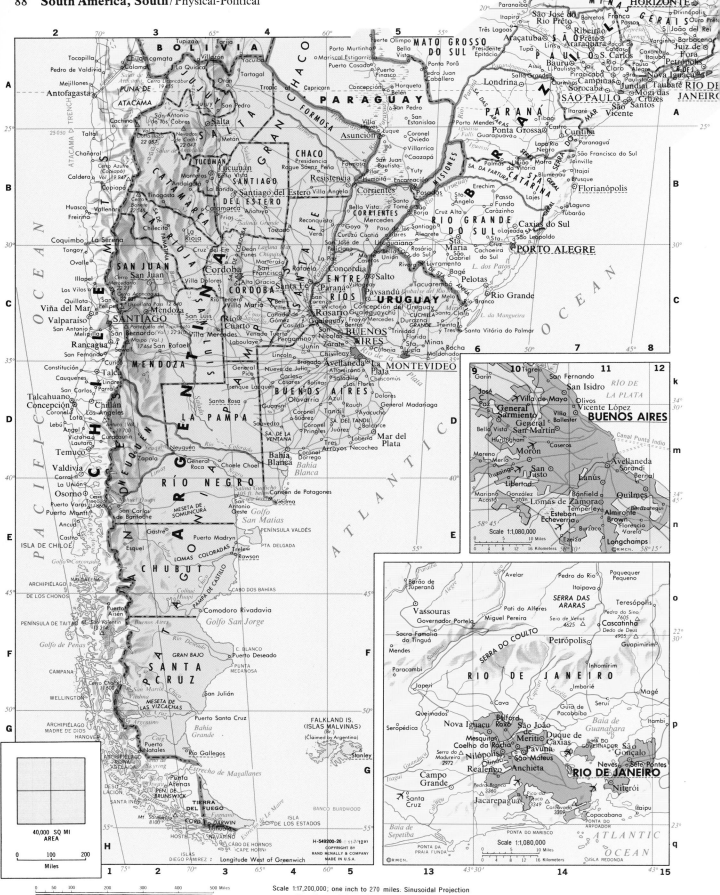

Scale 1:17,200,000; one inch to 270 miles. Sinusoidal Projection
Elevations and depressions are given in feet

Antarctica

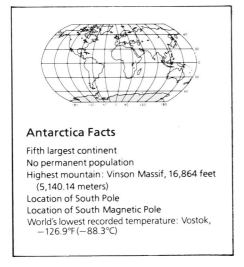

Antarctica Facts

Fifth largest continent
No permanent population
Highest mountain: Vinson Massif, 16,864 feet
    (5,140.14 meters)
Location of South Pole
Location of South Magnetic Pole
World's lowest recorded temperature: Vostok,
    −126.9°F (−88.3°C)

Antarctica, the coldest continent on earth, rests squarely on the South Pole. It is so cold here that an unprotected visitor would freeze in minutes. In midwinter, June, temperatures inland may drop below −100°F (−73°C).

Because of the tilt of the earth's axis and its path around the sun, Antarctica is without sunlight for months at a time. Even in "summer," the sun's rays strike at such a slanted angle the land receives very little heat.

Most of Antarctica is covered with snow heaped so thick it forms a mile-high plateau at the pole. Bitter winds shriek over the seemingly endless white sheet at speeds averaging forty-four miles (seventy-one kilometers) an hour. In many places the snow has been packed by its own weight and frozen to become a massive ice pack. This ice is so heavy it has pressed parts of the land well below sea level. If the ice cap melted, all that could be seen above the waters would be the peaks of the mountain chain which twists some 3,000 miles (4,827 kilometers) across the continent.

Many warm-blooded animals thrive in the waters on the fringes of the continent. Among these are seals, birds, and the great blue whales. Antarctica's largest land animal is a wingless insect less than one-tenth inch (2.54 millimeters) long.

Halfway between land and sea animals are Antarctica's penguins. Though penguins are birds, they cannot fly. Their wings are paddles that help them move underwater.

Surprisingly, Antarctica's waters hold more marine life than oceans in warmer parts of the globe. Antarctica's land has yielded small amounts of gold, iron, uranium, and coal. It is also thought to contain oil and natural gas.

Many nations claim parts of Antarctica. But the Antarctic Treaty of 1959 pledges these nations to wait until 1989 to settle their claims. Antarctica's future may well be more exciting than its lonely past.

Many nations have sent teams to Antarctica. Dog sleds are still used, but motorized toboggans are more common.

Glossary and List of Map and Geographical Terms

Air mass: a body of air a hundred to a thousand miles across and reaching several miles upward.

Altitude: the height above sea level of the earth's physical features.

Antarctic and Arctic zones: the bitterly cold areas surrounding the South and North poles.

Astrolabe: an instrument used to observe the stars' positions. Used before the invention of the sextant.

Atmosphere: the entire mass of air surrounding the planet Earth.

Atoll: the ring of coral around an ocean lagoon, all that remains after a volcanic island sinks into the sea.

Axis: an imaginary line between the poles. The earth turns around its axis every twenty-four hours.

Barometer: an instrument that measures the weight of the air.

Barren: any land area that lacks normal vegetation.

Basin: any land area drained by a river and its tributaries.

Beast of burden: an animal used to carry heavy materials or perform other heavy work.

Bush country: a large land area with little vegetation, usually thinly settled.

Butte: an isolated upraised land area with steep sides and a small top.

Canal: any artificial waterway.

Canyon: a deep valley with steep sides.

Cape: a point of land jutting out into water.

Cartographer: a mapmaker.

Chronometer: an instrument used by navigators for measuring time—east-west distances from the prime meridian.

Cirrus: a white wispy cloud formed at very high altitudes.

Coastal: land at the edge of the ocean or sea.

Compass: an instrument for telling direction. A magnetic needle turns freely on a pivot and points to the magnetic north.

Continent: one of the great named divisions of land on earth.

Continental shelf: a shallow undersea area bordering a continent, ending in a steep slope to the deeper ocean.

Contour line: a line on a map joining the land points having the same elevation, or height.

Coral reef: a rocklike deposit of animal skeletons just below the ocean surface.

Cumulus: a huge summer cloud with a flat base and high fluffy top.

Cyclone: a storm or system of winds spinning around a center of low atmospheric pressure.

Desert: dry land which supports only widely scattered plant and animal life.

Doldrums: an area of calm winds and warm updrafts near the equator.

Downdraft: a downward movement of air, as during a thunderstorm.

Earthquake: a shaking of the earth caused by volcanic or plate action.

Earth's crust: the earth's outer layers.

Earth tremor: a quivering on the surface of the earth.

Easterly: wind blowing from the east.

Elevation: the height to which earth features reach above sea level.

Equator: an imaginary line on globes and maps halfway between the poles.

Erosion: the wearing away or destruction of land by wind, water, and ice.

Export: to send a product to another country.

Extinct: no longer existing.

Eye of a storm: nearly calm center of a storm.

Fall line: a line along which rivers plunge from plateaus and hills to the plain below.

Fault: a fracture in the earth's crust.

Feature: an important, usually very noticeable, part of the earth.

Fertile: able to bear fruit or vegetables in great quantities.

Fjord: an ice-carved inlet of the sea between steep cliffs.

Frontal zone: an area of severe weather where two great air masses—one cold and one hot—collide.

Funnel: the funnel-shaped downward section of a storm cloud, particularly in a tornado.

Game preserve: an area where wild animals are protected.

Geologist: a scientist who studies the earth's outer layers.

Geyser: a natural spring that spouts hot water and steam.

Glacier: a large body of ice moving slowly down over an area of land.

Gravitational pull: that force which pulls objects toward itself.

Grid: a set of lines crossing each other on which maps are drawn.

Gulf: part of an ocean or sea reaching into a land area.

Habitat: the place where a plant or animal naturally lives and grows.

Headland: a point of high land jutting out into a body of water.

Hemisphere: half of the earth.

Hill: an upland area of gentle slopes and a broad summit, generally lower than a mountain.

Horse latitudes: about 30° north and 30° south. Areas of descending air and high pressures.

Hurricane: a tropical cyclone with winds of at least seventy-four miles (119.08 kilometers) per hour and heavy rain.

Ice cap: a cover of permanent ice and snow on the earth's surface.

Intermontane: between the mountains.

Island: land, smaller than a continent, surrounded by water.

Isthmus: a narrow strip of land joining two larger land areas.

Jungle: a mass of tropical plant growth.

Lagoon: a shallow pond near a larger body of water.

Landform: a feature of the earth's surface.

Landmark: an outstanding feature of the land used as a guide.

Landmass: a large area of land.

Latitude: the distance between parallels, north or south of the equator.

Lava: melted rock which flows out of the earth's surface.

Legend: key to the symbols and colors used on maps.

Longitude: the east-west distance between meridians.

Marine: having to do with the sea.

Marsupials: mammals whose young develop within pouches on the females' abdomens, such as kangaroos and opossums.

Mattang: stick chart used by Micronesian islanders 2,000 years ago to show ocean wave patterns.

Meridians: imaginary lines joining the North and South poles. The distance between meridians is called longitude.

Mesa: an isolated tableland with steeply sloping sides and a large flat land area on top.

Meteorologist: a scientist who studies the earth's atmosphere and forecasts the weather.

Microscopic: invisible to the naked eye unless magnified through a microscope.

Migrate: to move from one region or climate to another in order to survive.

Molten rock: rock turned into liquid by intense heat.

Monsoon: a seasonal wind in southern Asia.

Mountain: a landmass, with steep slopes and a sharp peak.

Natural barrier: any geographical feature which separates two areas.

Navigation: the science of moving around on—or above—the earth.

Nimbus: a dark rain cloud reaching as far as one can see.

Ocean: the whole body of saltwater covering nearly three-fourths of the earth's surface.

Oceanographer: a scientist who studies the sea and everything in it.

Outback: bush country and deserts, found in Australia.

Ozone: a special form of oxygen. High in the atmosphere, a layer of ozone surrounds the earth, screening out the sun's harmful rays. Closer to the earth's surface, ozone sometimes forms as the result of pollution. Even in small amounts, ozone is irritating to breathe.

Pampas: a grass-covered plain found in South America.

Parallels: imaginary lines circling the earth in an east-west direction. Like railroad tracks, they never meet. The distance between parallels is called latitude.

Peninsula: an area of land almost surrounded by water.

Physical: that which can be seen and measured and, perhaps, weighed. Things that have height and width and depth. A physical map shows the earth's major features—mountains, hills, plains, oceans, rivers, lakes.

Piedmont: the area lying or formed at the base of mountains. May consist of plateaus or low hills.

Plain: an area of level-to-rolling, almost treeless land.

Plankton: microscopic animal and plant life found in the sea.

Plateau: large level land area raised sharply above the surrounding land.

Plates: sections underlying the surface of the earth. Their movement may cause faults or other changes in the surface.

Polar: having to do with the North or South poles or the areas around them.

Portolan charts: detailed maps used for navigation by European sailors in the 1500s.

Prehistoric: the time before history was written down.

Prime meridian: the meridian chosen to be 0° or prime meridian. It passes through Greenwich, England.

Quake: to quiver or shake. A shortened term for earthquake. A tremor.

Rain forest: a densely grown tropical woodland with almost daily rainfall.

Range: a series of mountains in a group.

Rapid: part of a river where the current is fast and the surface is broken by large rocks.

Ridge: a long narrow upper crest. Can be of very high formations on mountains, hills, waves, even parts of the ocean floor.

Rift: a deep crack in the earth's crust.

Scale: a mathematical key which tells how much the earth or an area of the earth was reduced to fit on a map.

Sea: á saltwater body smaller than an ocean.

Sea level: the average level of the ocean between high tide and low tide. Land areas are measured above or below sea level.

Sedge: tufted marsh plants.

Seismologist: a scientist who studies earthquakes.

Silt: water-carried earth material, finer than sand.

Smog: a combination of fog and smoke.

Solar energy: power from the sun.

Solar system: the sun and the planets and other space objects which revolve around it.

Space orbit: a circular path outside the solar system.

Spillway: a passage for extra water to run over or around something that stands in its way.

Steppe: a vast level or rolling tract of treeless land.

Stratus: a wide flat cloud at a low altitude.

Subcontinent: a large peninsulalike area of land. For example, India.

Tectonic: having to do with changes in the shape of the earth's surface and the forces that produce those changes.

Terrain: the landscape.

Tornado: a destructive whirling cyclone over a land area.

Trade winds: the winds that blow out of the horse latitudes toward the doldrums. In the Northern Hemisphere they are the northeast trade winds; in the Southern Hemisphere they are the southeast trade winds.

Trench: a long, narrow, steep-sided ditch in the ocean floor.

Tropics: the area on both sides of the equator where temperatures are always high and rainfall is plentiful.

Tundra: a treeless plain in arctic regions. Areas below the surface are permanently frozen.

Updraft: an upward movement of air.

Upland: high land—mountains, hills, plateaus, mesas, buttes.

Valley: a low area between ranges of hills or mountains.

Volcanic cone: the top of a volcano.

Volcano: an opening in the earth's surface from which molten rock and steam erupt.

Volcanologist: a scientist who studies volcanoes.

Westerly: wind blowing from the west.

Map Names and Abbreviations

This table lists the names and the abbreviations used for features on the physical-political maps. Each entry includes the feature name, the language from which it comes, and, in the case of foreign names, its English translation. Abbreviations are shown for those names that are abbreviated on the maps.

Ákra (Greek): cape, *Akr.*

Cabo (Spanish, Portuguese): cape, *C.*

Cap (French): cape, *C.*

Cape (English): *C.*

Cerro (Spanish): mountain, hill

Cordillera (Spanish): mountain chain, *Cord.*

Erg (Arabic): strait

Estrecho (Spanish): strait

Fort (English): *Ft.*

Golfo (Spanish, Italian): gulf, bay, *G.*

Gora (Russian): mountain, *G.*

Gulf (English): *G.*

Hai (Chinese): sea

Île (French): island

Ilha (Portuguese): island

Isla (Spanish): island, *I.*

Jabal (Arabic): mountain

Khrebet (Russian): mountain range

Lake (English): *L.*

Lago (Spanish, Portuguese): lake, *L.*

More (Russian): sea

Mountain(s) (English): *Mt. (Mts.)*

Mys (Russian): cape, *M.*

National (English): *Nat'l*

Occidental (Spanish): western

Oriental (Spanish): eastern

Óros (Greek): mountain

Ozero (Russian): lake, *Oz.*

Peninsula (English): *Pen.*

Peski (Russian): desert

People's Democratic Republic (English): *P.D.R.*

Plato (Russian): plateau

Point (English): *Pt.*

Pointe (French): point, *Pte.*

Poluostrov (Russian): peninsula, *P-Ov.*

Proliv (Russian): strait

Punta (Spanish): point

Reservoir (English): *Res.*

Río (Spanish): river, *R.*

River (English): *R.*

Salto (Spanish, Portuguese): waterfall

Serra (Portuguese): mountain chain, *Sa.*

Shan (Chinese): mountain, hill

Sierra (Spanish): mountain range, *Sa.*

Sound (English): *Sd.*

Soviet Socialist Republic (English): *S.S.R.*

Vodokhranilishche (Russian): reservoir, *Vdkhr.*

Volcano (English): *Vol.*

World Facts and Comparisons

General Information

Equatorial diameter of the earth, 7,926.38 miles.
Polar diameter of the earth, 7,899.80 miles.
Mean diameter of the earth, 7,917.52 miles.
Equatorial circumference of the earth, 24,901.46 miles.
Polar circumference of the earth, 24,855.34 miles.
Mean distance from the earth to the sun, 93,020,000 miles.
Mean distance from the earth to the moon, 238,857 miles.
Total area of the earth, 197,000,000 square miles.

Highest elevation on the earth's surface, Mt. Everest, Asia, 29,028 feet.
Lowest elevation on the earth's land surface, shores of the Dead Sea, Asia, 1,312 feet below sea level.
Greatest known depth of the ocean, southwest of Guam, Pacific Ocean, 35,810 feet.
Total land area of the earth (incl. inland water and Antarctica), 57,800,000 square miles.

Area of Africa, 11,700,000 square miles.
Area of Antarctica, 5,400,000 square miles.
Area of Asia, 17,300,000 square miles.
Area of Europe, 3,800,000 square miles.
Area of North America, 9,400,000 square miles.
Area of Oceania (incl. Australia) 3,300,000 square miles.
Area of South America, 6,900,000 square miles.
Population of the earth (est.1/1/91), 5,350,000,000.

Principal Islands and Their Areas

ISLAND	Area (Sq. Mi.)
Baffin I., Can.	195,928
Banks I., Can.	27,038
Borneo (Kalimantan), Asia	287,300
Bougainville, Papua New Guinea	3,600
Cape Breton I., Can.	3,981
Celebes (Sulawesi), Indon.	73,057
Ceram (Seram), Indon.	45,801
Corsica, France	3,352
Crete, Greece	3,189
Cuba, N.A.	42,800
Cyprus, Asia	3,572
Devon I., Can.	21,331
Ellesmere I., Can.	75,767
Flores, Indon.	5,502
Great Britain, U.K.	88,795
Greenland, N.A.	840,000
Guadalcanal, Solomon Is.	2,060
Hainan Dao, China	13,100
Hawaii, U.S.	4,034
Hispaniola, N.A.	29,300
Hokkaidō, Japan	32,245
Honshū, Japan	89,176
Iceland, Europe	39,800
Ireland, Europe	32,600
Jamaica, N.A.	4,200
Java (Jawa), Indon.	51,038
Kodiak I., U.S.	3,670
Kyūshū, Japan	17,129
Leyte, Philippines	2,785
Long Island, U.S.	1,377
Luzon, Philippines	40,420
Madagascar, Africa	227,000
Melville I., Can.	16,274
Mindanao, Philippines	36,537
Mindoro, Philippines	3,759
Negros, Philippines	4,907
New Britain, Papua New Guinea	14,093
New Caledonia, Oceania	6,252
Newfoundland, Can.	42,031
New Guinea, Asia-Oceania	309,000
New Ireland, Papua New Guinea	3,500
North East Land, Norway	6,350
North I., New Zealand	44,274
Novaya Zemlya, Sov. Un.	31,900
Palawan, Philippines	4,550
Panay, Philippines	4,446
Prince of Wales I., Can.	12,872
Puerto Rico, N.A.	3,500
Sakhalin, Sov. Un.	29,500
Samar, Philippines	5,100
Sardinia, Italy	9,301
Shikoku, Japan	7,258
Sicily, Italy	9,926
Somerset I., Can.	9,570
Southampton I., Can.	15,913
South I., New Zealand	57,870
Spitsbergen, Norway	15,260
Sri Lanka, Asia	24,900
Sumatra (Sumatera), Indon.	182,860
Taiwan, Asia	13,900
Tasmania, Austl.	26,200
Tierra del Fuego, S.A.	18,600
Timor, Indon.	5,743
Vancouver I., Can.	12,079
Victoria I., Can.	83,897
Vrangelya (Wrangel), Sov. Un.	2,800

Principal Lakes, Oceans, Seas, and Their Areas

LAKE Country	Area (Sq. Mi.)
Arabian Sea,	1,492,000
Aral'skoye More, (Aral Sea) Sov. Un.	24,700
Arctic Ocean,	5,400,000
Athabasca, L., Can.	3,064
Atlantic Ocean,	31,800,000
Balkhash, Ozero, (L.) Sov. Un.	7,100
Baltic Sea, Eur.	163,000
Baykal, Ozero, (L. Baikal) Sov. Un.	12,200
Bering Sea, Asia-N.A.	876,000
Black Sea, Eur.-Asia	178,000
Caribbean Sea, N.A.-S.A.	1,063,000
Caspian Sea, Iran-Sov. Un.	143,240
Chad, L., Cameroon-Chad-Nig.	6,300
Erie, L., Can.-U.S.	9,910
Eyre, L., Austl.	3,700
Gairdner, L., Austl.	1,700
Great Bear Lake, Can.	12,095
Great Salt Lake, U.S.	1,680
Great Slave Lake, Can.	11,030
Hudson Bay, Can.	475,000
Huron, L., Can.-U.S.	23,000
Indian Ocean,	28,900,000
Japan, Sea of, Asia	389,000
Koko Nor, (Qinghai Hu) China	1,650
Ladozhskoye Ozero, (L. Ladoga) Sov. Un.	683
Manitoba, L., Can.	1,785
Mediterranean Sea, Eur.-Afr.-Asia	967,000
Mexico, Gulf of, N.A.	596,000
Michigan, L., U.S.	22,300
Nicaragua, Lago de, Nic.	3,150
North Sea, Eur.	222,000
Nyasa, L., Malawi-Mozambique-Tanz.	11,150
Onezhskoye Ozero, (L. Onega) Sov. Un.	3,753
Ontario, L., Can.-U.S.	7,540
Pacific Ocean,	63,800,000
Red Sea, Afr.-Asia	169,000
Rudolf, L., Ethiopia-Kenya	2,473
Superior, L., Can.-U.S.	31,700
Tanganyika, L., Afr.	12,350
Titicaca, Lago, Bol.-Peru	3,200
Torrens, L., Austl.	2,300
Vänern, (L.) Swe.	2,156
Van Gölü, (L.) Tur.	1,420
Victoria, L., Ken.-Tan.-Ug.	26,820
Winnipeg, L., Can.	9,416
Winnipegosis, L., Can.	2,075
Yellow Sea, China-Korea	480,000

Principal Mountains and Their Heights

MOUNTAIN Country	Elev. (Ft.)
Aconcagua, Cerro, Argentina	22,831
Annapurna, Nepal	26,504
Antofalla, Volcán, Argentina	20,013
Api, Nepal	23,399
Apo, Mt., Philippines	9,692
Ararat, Turkey	16,804
Ayers Rock, Australia	2,844
Barú, Volcán, Panama	11,410
Belukha, Gol'tsy, Soviet Union	14,783
Bia, Phu, Laos	9,252
Blanc, Mont, France-Italy	15,771
Blanca Pk., Colorado, U.S.	14,317
Bolívar (La Columna), Venezuela	16,411
Borah Pk., Idaho, U.S.	12,662
Cameroon Mtn., Cameroon	13,451
Carrauntoohil, Ireland	3,414
Chimborazo, Ecuador	20,561
Chirripó, Cerro, Costa Rica	12,530
Colima, Nevado de, Mexico	13,993
Cook, Mt., New Zealand	12,349
Cotopaxi, Ecuador	19,347
Cristóbal Colón, Pico, Colombia	19,029
Damāvand, Qolleh-ye, Iran	18,386
Dhaulāgiri, Nepal	26,810
Duarte, Pico, Dominican Rep.	10,417
Dychtau, gora, Soviet Union	17,073
Egmont, Mt., New Zealand	8,260
Elbert, Mt., Colorado, U.S.	14,431
El'brus, Gora, Soviet Union	18,510
Elgon, Mt., Kenya-Uganda	14,178
eNjesuthi, South Africa	11,306
Erciyeş Daği, Turkey	12,848
Etna, Mt., Italy	10,902
Everest, Mt., China-Nepal	29,028
Fairweather, Mt., Alaska-Canada	15,300
Finsteraarhorn, Switzerland	14,022
Foraker, Mt., Alaska, U.S.	17,400
Fuji-san, Japan	12,388
Gannett Pk., Wyoming, U.S.	13,785
Gasherbrum, China-Pakistan	26,470
Gerlachovský Stit, Czechoslovakia	8,710
Giluwe, Mt., Papua New Guinea	14,331
Glittertinden, Norway	8,110
Gongga Shan, China	24,790
Grand Teton Mtn., Wyoming, U.S.	13,766
Grossglockner, Austria	12,461
Gunnbjørn Fjeld, Greenland	12,139
Hadūr Shu'ayb, Yemen	12,336
Haleakala Crater, Hawaii, U.S.	10,025
Haltiatunturi, Finland-Norway	4,357
Hekla, Iceland	4,892
Hkakabo Razi, Burma	19,296
Hood, Mt., Oregon, U.S.	11,239
Huascarán, Nevado, Peru	22,205
Huila, Nevado de, Colombia	18,865
Hvannadalshnúkur, Iceland	6,952
Illampu, Nevado, Bolivia	20,873
Illimani, Nevado, Bolivia	21,151
Iztaccíhuatl, Mexico	17,343
Jaya, Puncak, Indonesia	16,503
Jungfrau, Switzerland	13,642
K2 (Godwin Austen), China-Pakistan	28,250
Kāmet, China-India	25,447
Kānchenjunga, India-Nepal	28,208
Karisimbi, Volcan, Rwanda-Zaire	14,787
Kātrīnā, Jabal, Egypt	8,668
Kebnekaise, Sweden	6,962
Kenya, Mt., Kenya	17,058
Kerinci, Gunung, Indonesia	12,467
Kilimanjaro, Tanzania	19,340
Kinabalu, Gunong, Malaysia	13,455
Klyuchevskaya, Soviet Union	15,584
Kommunizma, Pik, Soviet Union	24,590
Korab, Albania-Yugoslavia	9,026
Kosciusko, Mt., Australia	7,316
Koussi, Emi, Chad	11,204
Kula Kangri, Bhutan	24,784
Lassen Pk., California, U.S.	10,457
Llullaillaco, Volcán, Argentina-Chile	22,057
Logan, Mt., Canada	19,524
Longs Pk., Colorado, U.S.	14,255
Makālu, China-Nepal	27,825
Margherita Pk., Zaire-Uganda	16,763
Markham, Mt., Antarctica	14,272
Maromokotro, Madagascar	9,436
Matterhorn, Italy-Switzerland	14,692
Mauna Kea, Hawaii, U.S.	13,796
Mauna Loa, Hawaii, U.S.	13,680
McKinley, Mt., Alaska, U.S.	20,320
Meru, Mt., Tanzania	14,978
Misti, Volcán, Peru	19,098
Mitchell, Mt., North Carolina, U.S.	6,684
Moldoveanu, Romania	8,343
Mulhacén, Spain (continental)	11,424
Musala, Bulgaria	9,596
Muztag, China	25,338
Muztagata, China	24,757
Namjagbarwa Feng, China	25,446
Nanda Devi, India	25,645
Nānga Parbat, Pakistan	26,650
Narodnaya, Gora, Soviet Union	6,214
Neblina, Pico da, Brazil-Venezuela	9,888
Nevis, Ben, United Kingdom	4,406
Ojos del Salado, Nevado, Argentina-Chile	22,615
Ólimbos, Cyprus	6,401
Ólimbos, Greece	9,570
Orizaba, Pico de, Mexico	18,406
Orohena, Mont, French Polynesia	7,352
Paektu san, North Korea-China	9,003
Paricutín, Mexico	9,213
Parnassós, Greece	8,061
Pelée, Montagne, Martinique	4,800
Pico, Cape Verde	9,281
Pidurutalagala, Sri Lanka	8,281
Pikes Pk., Colorado, U.S.	14,110
Pissis, Monte, Argentina	22,241
Pobedy, pik, China-Soviet Union	24,406
Popocatépetl, Volcán, Mexico	17,887
Pulog, Mt., Philippines	9,606
Rainier, Mt., Washington, U.S.	14,410
Ras Dashen Terara, Ethiopia	15,158
Rinjani, Gunung, Indonesia	12,224
Rosa, Monte, Italy-Switzerland	15,203
Ruapehu, New Zealand	9,175
St. Elias, Mt., Alaska, U.S.-Canada	18,008
Sajama, Nevado, Bolivia	21,463
Sawdā', Qurnat as, Lebanon	10,114
Scafell Pikes, England, U.K.	3,210
Semeru, Gunung, Indonesia	12,060
Shām, Jabal ash, Oman	9,902
Shasta, Mt., California, U.S.	14,162
Snowdon, Wales, U.K.	3,560
Tahat, Algeria	9,541
Tajumulco (Vol.), Guatemala	13,816
Tirich Mīr, Pakistan	25,230
Tomanivi (Victoria), Fiji	4,341
Toubkal, Jebel, Morocco	13,665
Triglav, Yugoslavia	9,393
Trikora, Puncak, Indonesia	15,584
Tupungato, Portezuelo de, Argentina-Chile	22,310
Turquino, Pico de, Cuba	6,496
Vesuvio (Vesuvius), Italy	4,190
Victoria, Mt., Papua New Guinea	13,238
Vinson Massif, Antarctica	16,864
Waddington, Mt., Canada	13,260
Washington, Mt., New Hampshire, U.S.	6,288
Weisshorn, Switzerland	14,783
Whitney, Mt., California, U.S.	14,491
Wilhelm, Mt., Papua New Guinea	14,793
Wrangell, Mt., Alaska, U.S.	14,163
Xixabangma Feng (Gosainthan), China	26,286
Zugspitze, Austria-Germany	9,721

Principal Rivers and Their Lengths

RIVER Continent	Length (Mi.)
Albany, N.A.	610
Aldan, Asia	1,412
Amazonas-Ucayali, S.A.	4,000
Amu Darya, Asia	1,578
Amur, Asia	2,744
Amur-Argun, Asia	2,761
Araguaia, S.A.	1,400
Arkansas, N.A.	1,459
Athabasca, N.A.	765
Brahmaputra, Asia	1,770
Branco, S.A.	580
Brazos, N.A.	900
Canadian, N.A.	906
Churchill, N.A.	1,000
Colorado, N.A. (U.S.-Mex.)	1,450
Columbia, N.A.	1,200
Congo (Zaïre), Africa	2,900
Cumberland, N.A.	720
Danube, Europe	1,776
Darling, Australia	864
Dnepr, (Dnieper) Europe	1,400
Dnestr, (Dniestr) Europe	840
Don, Europe	1,162
Elbe, Europe	720
Euphrates, Asia	1,510
Fraser, N.A.	851
Ganges, Asia	1,560
Gila, N.A.	630
Godāvari, Asia	930
Green, N.A.	730
Huang, (Yellow) Asia	3,395
Indus, Asia	1,800
Irrawaddy, Asia	1,300
Juruá, S.A.	1,250
Kama, Europe	1,122
Kasai, Africa	1,338
Kolyma, Asia	1,323
Lena, Asia	2,700
Limpopo, Africa	1,100
Loire, Europe	625
Mackenzie, N.A.	2,635
Madeira, S.A.	2,013
Magdalena, S.A.	950
Marañón, S.A.	1,000
Mekong, Asia	2,600
Meuse, Europe	575
Mississippi, N.A.	2,348
Mississippi-Missouri, N.A.	3,740
Missouri, N.A.	2,315
Murray, Australia	1,566
Negro, S.A.	1,300
Neman, Europe	582
Niger, Africa	2,600
Nile, Africa	4,145
North Platte, N.A.	618
Ob'-Irtysh, Asia	3,362
Oder, Europe	565
Ohio, N.A.	981
Oka, Europe	900
Orange, Africa	1,300
Orinoco, S.A.	1,600
Ottawa, N.A.	790
Paraguay, S.A.	1,610
Paraná, S.A.	2,800
Parnaíba, S.A.	850
Peace, N.A.	1,195
Pechora, Europe	1,124
Pecos, N.A.	735
Pilcomayo, S.A.	1,550
Plata-Paraná, S.A.	3,030
Purús, S.A.	1,860
Red, N.A.	1,270
Rhine, Europe	820
Rhône, Europe	500
Rio Grande, N.A.	1,885
Roosevelt, S.A.	950
St. Lawrence, N.A.	800
Salado, S.A.	900
Salween, (Nu) Asia	1,750
São Francisco, S.A.	1,988
Saskatchewan-Bow, N.A.	1,205
Sava, Europe	585
Snake, N.A.	1,038
Sungari, (Songhua) Asia	1,140
Syr Dar'ya, Asia	1,370
Tagus, Europe	625
Tarim, Asia	1,328
Tennessee, N.A.	652
Tigris, Asia	1,180
Tisa, Europe	607
Tobol, Asia	989
Tocantins, S.A.	1,640
Ucayali, S.A.	1,220
Ural, Asia	1,509
Uruguay, S.A.	1,025
Verkhnyaya Tunguska, (Angara) Asia	1,105
Vilyuy, Asia	1,647
Volga, Europe	2,194
White, N.A. (Ar.-Mo.)	720
Wisła (Vistula), Europe	630
Xiang, Asia	930
Xingu, S.A.	1,230
Yangtze, (Chang) Asia	3,900
Yellowstone, N.A.	671
Yenisey, Asia	2,543
Yukon, N.A.	1,770
Zambezi, Africa	1,700

Principal Cities of the World

Abidjan, Ivory Coast	1,950,000
Accra, Ghana (1,250,000)	859,640
Addis Ababa, Ethiopia (1,760,000)	1,686,300
Adelaide, Australia (1,036,747)	12,340
Ahmadābād, India (2,400,000)	2,059,725
Aleppo (Halab), Syria (1,275,000)	1,261,000
Alexandria (Al Iskandarīyah), Egypt (3,350,000)	2,917,327
Algiers (El Djazaïr), Algeria (2,547,983)	1,507,241
Alma-Ata, Soviet Union (1,190,000)	1,128,000
'Ammān, Jordan (1,450,000)	936,300
Amsterdam, Netherlands (1,860,000)	696,500
Ankara (Angora), Turkey (2,650,000)	2,553,209
Anshan, China	1,330,000
Antwerp (Antwerpen), Belgium (1,100,000)	479,748
Asunción, Paraguay (700,000)	477,100
Athens (Athínai), Greece (3,027,331)	885,737
Atlanta, Georgia, U.S. (2,833,511)	394,017
Auckland, New Zealand (850,000)	149,046
Baghdād, Iraq	3,841,268
Baku, Soviet Union (2,020,000)	1,150,000
Baltimore, Maryland, U.S. (2,382,172)	736,014
Bandung, Indonesia (1,800,000)	1,633,000
Bangalore, India (2,950,000)	2,476,355
Bangkok (Krung Thep), Thailand (6,450,000)	5,716,779
Barcelona, Spain (4,040,000)	1,714,355
Beijing (Peking), China (7,200,000)	6,710,000
Beirut, Lebanon (1,675,000)	509,000
Belém, Brazil (1,200,000)	1,116,578
Belfast, N. Ireland, U.K. (685,000)	303,800
Belgrade (Beograd), Yugoslavia (1,400,000)	1,130,000
Belo Horizonte, Brazil (2,950,000)	2,114,429
Berlin, Germany (3,825,000)	3,352,848
Bilbao, Spain (985,000)	384,733
Birmingham, England, U.K. (2,675,000)	1,013,995
Bombay, India (9,950,000)	8,243,405
Bonn, Germany (570,000)	282,190
Boston, Massachusetts, U.S. (4,171,643)	574,283
Brasília, Brazil	1,567,709
Bremen, Germany (800,000)	535,058
Brisbane, Australia (1,273,511)	744,828
Brussels (Bruxelles), Belgium (2,385,000)	136,920
Bucharest (București), Romania (2,275,000)	1,989,823
Budapest, Hungary (2,565,000)	2,016,132
Buenos Aires, Argentina (10,750,000)	2,922,829
Buffalo, New York, U.S. (1,189,288)	328,123
Cairo (Al Qāhirah), Egypt (9,300,000)	6,052,836
Calcutta, India (11,100,000)	3,305,006
Cali, Colombia (1,400,000)	1,350,565
Canberra, Australia (271,362)	247,194
Cape Town, South Africa (1,790,000)	776,617
Caracas, Venezuela (3,600,000)	1,816,901
Cardiff, Wales, U.K. (625,000)	262,313
Casablanca, Morocco (2,475,000)	2,139,204
Changchun, China (2,000,000†)	1,822,000
Chelyabinsk, Soviet Union (1,325,000)	1,143,000
Chengdu, China (2,960,000†)	1,884,000
Chicago, Illinois, U.S. (8,065,633)	2,783,726
Chittagong, Bangladesh (1,391,877)	980,000
Chongqing (Chungking), China (2,890,000†)	2,502,000
Cincinnati, Ohio, U.S. (1,744,124)	364,040
Cleveland, Ohio, U.S. (2,759,823)	505,616
Cologne (Köln), Germany (1,760,000)	937,482
Colombo, Sri Lanka (2,050,000)	683,000
Columbus, Ohio, U.S. (1,377,419)	632,910
Copenhagen (København), Denmark (1,685,000)	466,723
Curitiba, Brazil (1,700,000)	1,279,205
Dakar, Senegal	1,447,642
Dalian (Lüda), China	2,280,000
Dallas, Texas, U.S. (3,885,415)	1,006,877
Damascus (Dimashq), Syria (1,950,000)	1,326,000
Dar es Salaam, Tanzania	1,300,000
Delhi, India (7,200,000)	4,884,234
Denver, Colorado, U.S. (1,848,319)	467,610
Detroit, Michigan, U.S. (4,665,236)	1,027,974
Dhaka (Dacca), Bangladesh (3,430,312)	2,365,695
Dnepropetrovsk, Soviet Union (1,600,000)	1,179,000
Donetsk, Soviet Union (2,200,000)	1,110,000
Dresden, Germany (670,000)	518,057
Dublin (Baile Átha Cliath), Ireland (1,140,000)	502,749
Durban, South Africa (1,550,000)	634,301
Düsseldorf, Germany (1,190,000)	569,641
Edinburgh, Scotland, U.K. (630,000)	433,200
Essen, Germany (4,950,000)	620,594
Florence (Firenze), Italy (640,000)	425,835
Fortaleza, Brazil (1,825,000)	1,582,414
Frankfurt am Main, Germany (1,855,000)	625,258
Fukuoka, Japan (1,750,000)	1,160,440
Fushun, China	1,290,000
Gdańsk (Danzig), Poland (909,000)	461,500
Geneva (Génève), Switzerland (460,000)	165,404
Genoa (Genova), Italy (805,000)	727,427
Glasgow, Scotland, U.K. (1,800,000)	695,630
Guadalajara, Mexico (2,325,000)	1,626,152
Guangzhou (Canton), China (3,420,000†)	3,100,000
Guatemala, Guatemala (1,400,000)	1,057,210
Guayaquil, Ecuador (1,580,000)	1,572,615
Hamburg, Germany (2,225,000)	1,603,070
Hannover, Germany (1,000,000)	498,495
Hanoi, Vietnam (1,500,000)	1,089,000
Harare, Zimbabwe (890,000)	681,000
Harbin, China	2,710,000
Hartford, Connecticut, U.S. (1,085,837)	139,739
Havana (La Habana), Cuba (2,125,000)	2,036,800
Helsinki, Finland (1,040,000)	490,034
Hiroshima, Japan (1,575,000)	1,044,118
Ho Chi Minh City (Saigon), Vietnam (3,600,000)	3,169,000
Hong Kong, Hong Kong (4,770,000)	1,175,860
Honolulu, Hawaii, U.S. (836,231)	365,272
Houston, Texas, U.S. (3,711,043)	1,630,553
Hyderābād, India (2,750,000)	2,187,262
Ibadan, Nigeria	1,144,000
Indianapolis, Indiana, U.S. (1,249,822)	731,327
Irkutsk, Soviet Union	626,000
İstanbul, Turkey (7,550,000)	6,748,435
İzmir, Turkey (1,900,000)	1,762,849
Jakarta, Indonesia (10,000,000)	9,200,000
Jerusalem, Israel (530,000)	493,500
Jiddah, Saudi Arabia	1,300,000
Jinan, China (2,140,000†)	1,546,000
Johannesburg, South Africa (3,650,000)	632,369
Kābul, Afghanistan	1,424,400
Kānpur, India (1,875,000)	1,481,789
Kansas City, Missouri, U.S. (1,566,280)	435,146
Kaohsiung, Taiwan (1,845,000)	1,342,797
Karāchi, Pakistan (5,300,000)	4,901,627
Kathmandu, Nepal (320,000)	235,160
Katowice, Poland (2,778,000)	365,800
Kawasaki, Japan (*Tōkyō)	1,088,624
Kazan', Soviet Union (1,140,000)	1,094,000
Khar'kov, Soviet Union (1,940,000)	1,611,000
Khartoum (Al Kharṭūm), Sudan (1,450,000)	476,218
Kiev, Soviet Union (2,900,000)	2,587,000
Kingston, Jamaica (770,000)	646,400
Kinshasa, Zaire	3,000,000
Kitakyūshū, Japan (1,525,000)	1,056,402
Kōbe, Japan (*Ōsaka)	1,410,834
Kowloon, Hong Kong (*Hong Kong)	774,781
Kuala Lumpur, Malaysia (1,475,000)	919,610
Kunming, China (1,550,000†)	1,310,000
Kuwait (Al Kuwayt), Kuwait (1,375,000)	44,335
Kyōto, Japan (*Ōsaka)	1,479,218
Lagos, Nigeria (3,800,000)	1,213,000
Lahore, Pakistan (3,025,000)	2,707,215
Lanzhou, China (1,420,000†)	1,297,000
La Paz, Bolivia	992,592
Leeds, England, U.K. (1,540,000)	445,242
Leipzig, Germany (700,000)	545,307
Liège, Belgium (750,000)	200,891
Lille, France (1,020,000)	168,424
Lima, Peru (4,608,010)	371,122
Lisbon (Lisboa), Portugal (2,250,000)	807,167
Liverpool, England, U.K. (1,525,000)	538,809
Łódź, Poland (1,061,000)	851,500
London, England, U.K. (11,100,000)	6,574,009
Los Angeles, California, U.S. (14,531,529)	3,485,398
Louisville, Kentucky, U.S. (952,662)	269,063
Luanda, Angola	1,459,900
Lucknow, India (1,060,000)	895,721
Lyon, France (1,275,000)	413,095
Madras, India (4,475,000)	3,276,622
Madrid, Spain (4,650,000)	3,102,846
Managua, Nicaragua	682,000
Manchester, England, U.K. (2,775,000)	437,612
Manila, Philippines (6,800,000)	1,587,000
Mannheim, Germany (1,400,000)	300,468
Maracaibo, Venezuela	890,643
Marseille, France (1,225,000)	874,436
Mecca (Makkah), Saudi Arabia	550,000
Medan, Indonesia	2,110,000
Medellín, Colombia (2,095,000)	1,468,089
Melbourne, Australia (3,039,100)	55,300
Memphis, Tennessee, U.S. (981,747)	610,337
Mexico City, Mexico (14,100,000)	8,831,079
Miami, Florida, U.S. (3,192,582)	358,548
Milan (Milano), Italy (3,750,000)	1,495,260
Milwaukee, Wisconsin, U.S. (1,607,183)	628,088
Minneapolis, Minnesota, U.S. (2,464,124)	368,383
Minsk, Soviet Union (1,650,000)	1,589,000
Monterrey, Mexico (2,015,000)	1,090,009
Montevideo, Uruguay (1,550,000)	1,251,647
Montréal, Canada (2,921,357)	1,015,420
Moscow (Moskva), Soviet Union (13,100,000)	8,769,000
Munich (München), Germany (1,955,000)	1,211,617
Nagoya, Japan (4,800,000)	2,116,381
Nāgpur, India (1,302,066)	1,219,461
Nairobi, Kenya	1,505,000
Nanjing, China	2,390,000
Naples (Napoli), Italy (2,875,000)	1,204,211
Netzahualcóyotl, Mexico (*Mexico City)	1,341,230
Newcastle upon Tyne, England, U.K. (1,300,000)	199,064
New Delhi, India (*Delhi)	273,036
New Kowloon, Hong Kong (*Hong Kong)	1,526,910
New Orleans, Louisiana, U.S. (1,238,816)	496,938
New York, New York, U.S. (18,087,251)	7,322,564
Nizhniy Novgorod, Soviet Union (2,005,000)	1,425,000
Novosibirsk, Soviet Union (1,600,000)	1,436,000
Nürnberg, Germany (1,030,000)	480,078
Odessa, Soviet Union (1,185,000)	1,115,000
Oklahoma City, Oklahoma, U.S. (958,839)	444,719
Omsk, Soviet Union (1,175,000)	1,148,000
Ōsaka, Japan (16,450,000)	2,636,249
Oslo, Norway (720,000)	452,415
Ottawa, Canada (819,263)	300,763
Panamá, Panama (770,000)	411,549
Paris, France (9,775,000)	2,078,900
Perm', Soviet Union (1,160,000)	1,091,000
Perth, Australia (1,158,387)	82,413
Philadelphia, Pennsylvania, U.S. (5,899,345)	1,585,577
Phnum Pénh (Phnom Penh), Cambodia	700,000
Phoenix, Arizona, U.S. (2,122,101)	983,403
Pittsburgh, Pennsylvania, U.S. (2,242,798)	369,879
Port-au-Prince, Haiti (880,000)	797,000
Portland, Oregon, U.S. (1,477,895)	437,319
Porto (Oporto), Portugal (1,225,000)	327,368
Porto Alegre, Brazil (2,600,000)	1,272,121
Prague (Praha), Czechoslovakia (1,325,000)	1,215,656
Pretoria, South Africa (960,000)	443,059
Providence, Rhode Island, U.S. (1,141,510)	160,728
Pune, India (1,775,000)	1,203,351
Pusan, South Korea (3,800,000)	3,773,000
P'yŏngyang, North Korea (1,600,000)	1,283,000
Qingdao, China	1,300,000
Qiqihar, China (1,330,000†)	1,180,000
Québec, Canada (603,267)	164,580
Quezon City, Philippines (*Manila)	1,632,000
Quito, Ecuador (1,300,000)	1,137,705
Rabat, Morocco (980,000)	518,616
Rangoon (Yangon), Burma (2,800,000)	2,705,039
Rāwalpindi, Pakistan (1,040,000)	457,091
Recifé, Brazil (2,625,000)	1,287,623
Rīga, Latvia (1,005,000)	915,000
Rio de Janerio, Brazil (10,150,000)	5,603,388
Riyadh, Saudi Arabia	1,250,000
Rome (Roma), Italy (3,175,000)	2,815,457
Rosario, Argentina (1,045,000)	938,120
Rostov-na-Donu, Soviet Union (1,165,000)	1,020,000
Rotterdam, Netherlands (1,110,000)	576,300
St. Louis, Missouri, U.S. (2,444,099)	396,685
St. Paul, Minnesota, U.S. (*Minneapolis)	272,235
St. Petersburg (Leningrad), Soviet Union (5,750,000)	4,393,000
Salt Lake City, Utah, U.S. (1,072,227)	159,936
Salvador, Brazil (2,050,000)	1,804,438
Samara, Soviet Union (1,510,000)	1,280,000
San Antonio, Texas, U.S. (1,302,099)	935,933
San Diego, California, U.S. (2,949,000)	1,110,549
San Francisco, California, U.S. (6,253,311)	723,959
San José, Costa Rica (670,000)	278,600
San Juan, Puerto Rico (1,775,260)	424,600
San Salvador, El Salvador (920,000)	462,652
Santa Fe de Bogotá, Colombia (4,550,000)	4,260,000
Santiago, Chile (4,100,000)	232,667
Santo Domingo, Dominican Rep.	1,313,172
São Paulo, Brazil (15,175,000)	10,063,110
Sapporo, Japan (1,900,000)	1,542,979
Saratov, Soviet Union (1,155,000)	905,000
Seattle, Washington, U.S. (2,559,164)	516,259
Seoul (Sŏul), South Korea (15,850,000)	10,522,000
Shanghai, China (9,300,000)	7,220,000
Shenyang (Mukden), China (4,370,000†)	3,910,000
Singapore, Singapore (3,025,000)	2,685,400
Sofia (Sofiya), Bulgaria (1,205,000)	1,119,152
Stockholm, Sweden (1,550,000)	672,187
Stuttgart, Germany (1,925,000)	562,658
Surabaya, Indonesia	2,345,000
Sydney, Australia (3,623,550)	9,800
Taegu, South Korea	2,207,000
T'aipei, Taiwan (6,130,000)	2,637,100
Taiyuan, China (1,980,000†)	1,700,000
Tashkent, Soviet Union (2,325,000)	2,073,000
Tbilisi, Soviet Union (1,460,000)	1,260,000
Tegucigalpa, Honduras	551,606
Tehrān, Iran (7,500,000)	6,042,584
Tel Aviv-Yafo, Israel (1,735,000)	317,800
The Hague ('s-Gravenhage), Netherlands (770,000)	443,900
Tianjin (Tientsin), China (5,540,000†)	4,950,000
Tiranë, Albania	255,700
Tōkyō, Japan (27,700,000)	8,354,615
Toronto, Canada (3,427,168)	612,289
Tripoli (Tarābulus), Libya	990,697
Tunis, Tunisia (1,225,000)	596,654
Turin (Torino), Italy (1,550,000)	1,035,565
Ufa, Soviet Union (1,100,000)	1,083,000
Ulan Bator, Mongolia	548,400
Valencia, Spain (1,270,000)	743,933
Valparaíso, Chile (675,000)	265,355
Vancouver, Canada (1,380,729)	431,147
Venice (Venezia), Italy (420,000)	88,700
Vienna (Wien), Austria (1,875,000)	1,482,800
Vladivostok, Soviet Union	648,000
Volgograd (Stalingrad), Soviet Union (1,360,000)	999,000
Warsaw (Warszawa), Poland (2,323,000)	1,651,200
Washington, D.C., U.S. (3,923,574)	609,909
Wellington, New Zealand (350,000)	137,495
Winnipeg, Canada (625,304)	594,551
Wuhan, China	3,570,000
Wuppertal, Germany (830,000)	371,283
Xi'an, China (2,580,000†)	2,210,000
Yekaterinburg, Soviet Union (1,575,000)	1,331,000
Yerevan, Soviet Union (1,315,000)	1,199,000
Yokohama, Japan (*Tōkyō)	2,992,926
Zagreb, Yugoslavia	697,925
Zhengzhou, China (1,580,000†)	1,150,000
Zurich, Switzerland (860,000)	342,861

Metropolitan area populations are shown in parentheses.
*City is located within the metropolitan area of another city; for example, Kyōto, Japan is located in the Ōsaka metropolitan area.
†Population of entire municipality or district, including rural area.

Index of Major Places on the Physical-Political Maps

Each entry in this index reference system consists of a place-name, a political-division name, or a physical-feature name; a map key; and a map page number. For specific instructions on the use of map keys, see page 19.

Each place-name is indexed to its city symbol on the map. Each political division, such as a state, is indexed to the location of its name on the map. Each physical feature, such as a river, is also indexed to the location of its name.

Following each name is the name of the country in which the feature is located. However, some physical features extend into two or more countries. In this case, the continent is listed.

In some entries, an alternate name is given in parentheses. This is the name used locally for that place, or a previously used name.

A small, or lowercase, letter in a map key means that place is keyed to an inset map rather than to the main map on the page. Two map keys are shown for areas that begin on one map and continue on another map.

A standard alphabetizing system is used in this index. If more than one name has the same spelling, place-names are listed first, political divisions second, and physical features third.